Level 1

¡Avancemos!

Unit 7 Resource Book

HOLT McDOUGAL
a division of Houghton Mifflin Harcourt

Fine Art Acknowledgments

Page 86 *Colores simples* (1999), Daniel Kaplan. Oil on canvas, 70 cm x 100 cm. Courtesy of Galería Zurbarán, Buenos Aires, Argentina.

Page 87 *Sarita* (1947), Raúl Soldi. Oil on canvas, 74 cm x 123 cm. Courtesy of Fundación Soldi.

Page 88 *Mañana de sol* (1966), Benito Quinquela Martín. Oleo sobre aglomerado, 77 cm x 87 cm. Courtesy of Galería Zurbarán, Buenos Aires.

Page 89 *De mi Buenos Aires* (1996), Norberto Russo. Oil on canvas, Galería Zurbarán, Buenos Aires, Galería Zurbarán/SuperStock.

ISBN-13: 978-0-618-76618-5
ISBN-10: 0-618-76618-9   12 13   1689   16 15
4500531933
Internet: www.holtmcdougal.com

HOLT McDOUGAL

¡Avancemos!

Table of Contents

To the Teacher

Welcome to *¡Avancemos!* This exciting new Spanish program from McDougal Littell has been designed to provide you—the teacher of today's foreign language classroom—with comprehensive pedagogical support.

PRACTICE WITH A PURPOSE

Activities throughout the program begin by establishing clear goals. Look for the **¡Avanza!** arrow that uses student-friendly language to lead the way towards achievable goals. Built-in self-checks in the student text (**Para y piensa:** Did you get it?) offer the chance to assess student progress throughout the lesson. Both the student text and the workbooks offer abundant leveled practice to match varied student needs.

CULTURE AS A CORNERSTONE

¡Avancemos! celebrates the cultural diversity of the Spanish-speaking world by motivating students to think about similarities and contrasts among different Spanish-speaking cultures. Essential questions encourage thoughtful discussion and comparison between different cultures.

LANGUAGE LEARNING THAT LASTS

The program presents topics in manageable chunks that students will be able to retain and recall. "Recycle" topics are presented frequently so students don't forget material from previous lessons. Previously learned content is built upon and reinforced across the different levels of the program.

TIME-SAVING TEACHER TOOLS

Simplify your planning with McDougal Littell's exclusive teacher resources: the all-inclusive EasyPlanner DVD-ROM, ready-made Power Presentations, and the McDougal Littell Assessment System.

Unit Resource Book

Each Unit Resource Book supports a unit of *¡Avancemos!* The Unit Resource Books provide a wide variety of materials to support, practice, and expand on the material in the *¡Avancemos!* student text.

Components **Following is a list of components included in each Unit Resource Book:**

BACK TO SCHOOL RESOURCES (UNIT 1 ONLY)

Review and start-up activities to support the **Lección preliminar** of the textbook.

DID YOU GET IT? RETEACHING & PRACTICE COPYMASTERS

 If students' performance on the **Para y piensa** self-check for a section does not meet your expectations, consider assigning the corresponding Did You Get It? Reteaching and Practice Copymasters. These copymasters provide extensive reteaching and additional practice for every vocabulary and grammar presentation section in *¡Avancemos!* Each vocabulary and grammar section has a corresponding three-page copymaster. The first page of the copymaster reteaches the subject material in a fresh manner. Immediately following this presentation page are two pages of practice exercises that help the student master the topic. The practice pages have engaging contexts and structures to retain students' attention.

PRACTICE GAMES

These games provide fun practice of the vocabulary and grammar just taught. They are targeted in scope so that each game practices a specific area of the **lesson**: *Práctica de vocabulario, Vocabulario en contexto, Práctica de gramática, Gramática en contexto, Todo junto, Repaso de la lección*, and the lesson's cultural information.

Video and audio resources

VIDEO ACTIVITIES

These two-page copymasters accompany the Vocabulary Video and each scene of the **Telehistoria** in Levels 1 and 2 and the **Gran desafío** in Level 3. The pre-viewing activity asks students to activate prior knowledge about a theme or subject related to the scene they will watch. The viewing activity is a simple activity for students to complete as they watch the video. The post-viewing activity gives students the opportunity to demonstrate comprehension of the video episode.

VIDEO SCRIPTS

This section provides the scripts of each video feature in the unit.

AUDIO SCRIPTS

This section contains scripts for all presentations and activities that have accompanying audio in the student text as well as in the two workbooks (*Cuaderno: práctica por niveles* and *Cuaderno para hispanohablantes*) and the assessment program.

Culture resources

MAP/CULTURE ACTIVITIES

This section contains a copymaster with geography and culture activities based on the Unit Opener in the textbook.

FINE ART ACTIVITIES

The fine art activities in every lesson ask students to analyze pieces of art that have been selected as representative of the unit location country. These copymasters can be used in conjunction with the full-color fine art transparencies in the Unit Transparency Book.

Home-school connection

FAMILY LETTERS & FAMILY INVOLVEMENT ACTIVITIES

This section is designed to help increase family support of the students' study of Spanish. The family letter keeps families abreast of the class's progress, while the family involvement activities let students share their Spanish language skills with their families in the context of a game or fun activity.

ABSENT STUDENT COPYMASTERS

The Absent Student Copymasters enable students who miss part of a **lesson** to go over the material on their own. The checkbox format allows teachers to choose and indicate exactly what material the student should complete. The Absent Student Copymasters also offer strategies and techniques to help students understand new or challenging information.

Core Ancillaries in the ¡Avancemos! Program

Leveled workbooks

CUADERNO: PRÁCTICA POR NIVELES

This core ancillary is a leveled practice workbook to supplement the student text. It is designed for use in the classroom or as homework. Students who can complete the activities correctly should be able to pass the quizzes and tests. Practice is organized into three levels of difficulty, labeled A, B, and C. Level B activities are designed to practice vocabulary, grammar, and other core concepts at a level appropriate to most of your students. Students who require more structure can complete Level A activities, while students needing more of a challenge should be encouraged to complete the activities in Level C. Each level provides a different degree of linguistic support, yet requires students to know and handle the same vocabulary and grammar content.

The following sections are included in *Cuaderno: práctica por niveles* for each **lesson**:

Vocabulario A, B, C	Escuchar A, B, C
Gramática 1 A, B, C	Leer A, B, C
Gramática 2 A, B, C	Escribir A, B, C
Integración: Hablar	Cultura A, B, C
Integración: Escribir	

CUADERNO PARA HISPANOHABLANTES

This core ancillary provides leveled practice for heritage learners of Spanish. Level A is for heritage learners who hear Spanish at home but who may speak little Spanish themselves. Level B is for those who speak some Spanish but don't read or write it yet and who may lack formal education in Spanish. Level C is for heritage learners who have had some formal schooling in Spanish. These learners can read and speak Spanish, but may need further development of their writing skills. The *Cuaderno para hispanohablantes* will ensure that heritage learners practice the same basic grammar, reading, and writing skills taught in the student text. At the same time, it offers additional instruction and challenging practice designed specifically for students with prior knowledge of Spanish.

The following sections are included in *Cuaderno para hispanohablantes* for each **lesson**:

Vocabulario A, B, C	Integración: Hablar
Vocabulario adicional	Integración: Escribir
Gramática 1 A, B, C	Lectura A, B, C
Gramática 2 A, B, C	Escritura A, B, C
Gramática adicional	Cultura A, B, C

Other Ancillaries

ASSESSMENT PROGRAM

For each level of *¡Avancemos!*, there are four complete assessment options. Every option assesses students' ability to use the lesson and unit vocabulary and grammar, as well as assessing reading, writing, listening, speaking, and cultural knowledge. The on-level tests are designed to assess the language skills of most of your students. Modified tests provide more support, explanation and scaffolding to enable students with learning difficulties to produce language at the same level as their peers. Pre-AP* tests build the test-taking skills essential to success on Advanced Placement tests. The assessments for heritage learners are all in Spanish, and take into account the strengths that native speakers bring to language learning.

In addition to leveled lesson and unit tests, there is a complete array of vocabulary, culture, and grammar quizzes. All tests include scoring rubrics and point teachers to specific resources for remediation.

UNIT TRANSPARENCY BOOKS—1 PER UNIT

Each transparency book includes:

- Map Atlas Transparencies (Unit 1 only)
- Unit Opener Map Transparencies
- Fine Art Transparencies
- Vocabulary Transparencies
- Grammar Presentation Transparencies
- Situational Transparencies with Label Overlay (plus student copymasters)
- Warm Up Transparencies
- Student Book and Workbook Answer Transparencies

LECTURAS PARA TODOS

A workbook-style reader, *Lecturas para todos*, offers all the readings from the student text as well as additional literary readings in an interactive format. In addition to the readings, they contain reading strategies, comprehension questions, and tools for developing vocabulary.

There are four sections in each *Lecturas para todos*:

- *¡Avancemos!* readings with annotated skill-building support
- *Literatura adicional*—additional literary readings
- Academic and Informational Reading Development
- Test Preparation Strategies

LECTURAS PARA HISPANOHABLANTES

Lecturas para hispanohablantes offers additional cultural readings for heritage learners and a rich selection of literary readings. All readings are supported by reading strategies, comprehension questions, tools for developing vocabulary, plus tools for literary analysis.

There are four sections in each *Lecturas para hispanohablantes*:

- *En voces* cultural readings with annotated skill-building support

- *Literatura adicional*—high-interest readings by prominent authors from around the Spanish-speaking world. Selections were chosen carefully to reflect the diversity of experiences Spanish-speakers bring to the classroom.

- Bilingual Academic and Informational Reading Development

- Bilingual Test Preparation Strategies, for success on standardized tests in English

COMIC BOOKS

These fun, motivating comic books are written in a contemporary, youthful style with full-color illustrations. Each comic uses the target language students are learning. There is one 32-page comic book for each level of the program.

TPRS: TEACHING PROFICIENCY THROUGH READING AND STORYTELLING

This book includes an up-to-date guide to TPRS and TPRS stories written by Piedad Gutiérrez that use *¡Avancemos!* lesson-specific vocabulary.

MIDDLE SCHOOL RESOURCE BOOK

- Practice activities to support the 1b Bridge lesson

- Diagnostic and Bridge Unit Tests

- Transparencies
    - Vocabulary Transparencies
    - Grammar Transparencies
    - Answer Transparencies for the Student Text
    - Bridge Warm Up Transparencies

- Audio CDs

LESSON PLANS

- Lesson Plans with suggestions for modifying instruction
- Core and Expansion options clearly noted
- IEP suggested modifications
- Substitute teacher lesson plans

BEST PRACTICES TOOLKIT

Strategies for Effective Teaching

- Research-based Learning Strategies
- Language Learning that Lasts: Teaching for Long-term Retention
- Culture as a Cornerstone/Cultural Comparisons
- English Grammar Connection
- Building Vocabulary
- Developing Reading Skills
- Differentiation
- Best Practices in Teaching Heritage Learners
- Assessment (including Portfolio Assessment, Reteaching and Remediation)
- Best Practices Swap Shop: Favorite Activities for Teaching Reading, Writing, Listening, Speaking
- Reading, Writing, Listening, and Speaking Strategies in the World Languages classroom
- ACTFL Professional Development Articles
- Thematic Teaching
- Best Practices in Middle School

Using Technology in the World Languages Classroom
Tools for Motivation

- Games in the World Languages Classroom
- Teaching Proficiency through Reading and Storytelling
- Using Comic Books for Motivation

Pre-AP and International Baccalaureate

- International Baccalaureate
- Pre-AP

Graphic Organizer Transparencies

- Teaching for Long-term Retention
- Teaching Culture
- Building Vocabulary
- Developing Reading Skills

Absent Student Copymasters—Tips for Students

LISTENING TO CDS AT HOME

- Open your text, workbook, or class notes to the corresponding pages that relate to the audio you will listen to. Read the assignment directions if there are any. Do these steps before listening to the audio selections.

- Listen to the CD in a quiet place. Play the CD loudly enough so that you can hear everything clearly. Keep focused. Play a section several times until you understand it. Listen carefully. Repeat aloud with the CD. Try to sound like the people on the CD. Stop the CD when you need to do so.

- If you are lost, stop the CD. Replay it and look at your notes. Take a break if you are not focusing. Return and continue after a break. Work in short periods of time: 5 or 10 minutes at a time so that you remain focused and energized.

QUESTION/ANSWER SELECTIONS

- If there is a question/answer selection, read the question aloud several times. Write down the question. Highlight the key words, verb endings, and any new words. Look up new words and write their meaning. Then say everything aloud.

- One useful strategy for figuring out questions is to put parentheses around groups of words that go together. For example: (¿Cuántos niños)(van)(al estadio)(a las tres?) Read each group of words one at a time. Check for meaning. Write out answers. Highlight key words and verb endings. Say the question aloud. Read the answer aloud. Ask yourself if you wrote what you meant.

- Be sure to say everything aloud several times before moving on to the next question. Check for spelling, verb endings, and accent marks.

FLASHCARDS FOR VOCABULARY

- If you have Internet access, go to ClassZone at classzone.com. All the vocabulary taught in *¡Avancemos!* is available on electronic flashcards. Look for the flashcards in the *¡Avancemos!* section of ClassZone.

- If you don't have Internet access, write the Spanish word or phrase on one side of a 3″×5″ card, and the English translation on the other side. Illustrate your flashcards when possible. Be sure to highlight any verb endings, accent marks, or other special spellings that will need a bit of extra attention.

GRAMMAR ACTIVITIES

- Underline or highlight all verb endings and adjective agreements. For example:
  Nosotros comemos pollo rico.

- Underline or highlight infinitive endings: **trabajar**.

- Underline or highlight accented letters. Say aloud and be louder on the accented letters. Listen carefully for the loudness. This will remind you where to write your accent mark. For example: **lápiz, lápices, árbol, árboles**

- When writing a sentence, be sure to ask yourself, "What do I mean? What am I trying to say?" Then check your sentence to be sure that you wrote what you wanted to say.

- Mark patterns with a highlighter. For example, for stem-changing verbs, you can draw a "boot" around the letters that change:

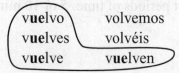

READING AND CULTURE SECTIONS

- Read the strategy box. Copy the graphic organizer so you can fill it out as you read.

- Look at the title and subtitles before you begin to read. Then look at and study any photos and read the captions. Translate the captions only if you can't understand them at all. Before you begin to read, guess what the selection will be about. What do you think that you will learn? What do you already know about this topic?

- Read any comprehension questions before beginning to read the paragraphs. This will help you focus on the upcoming reading selection. Copy the questions and highlight key words.

- Reread one or two of the questions and then go to the text. Begin to read the selection carefully. Read it again. On a sticky note, write down the appropriate question number next to where the answer lies in the text. This will help you keep track of what the questions have asked you and will help you focus when you go back to reread it later, perhaps in preparation for a quiz or test.

- Highlight any new words. Make a list or flashcards of new words. Look up their meanings. Study them. Quiz yourself or have a partner quiz you. Then go back to the comprehension questions and check your answers from memory. Look back at the text if you need to verify your answers.

PAIRED PRACTICE EXERCISES

- If there is an exercise for partners, practice both parts at home.
- If no partner is available, write out both scripts and practice both roles aloud. Highlight and underline key words, verb endings, and accent marks.

WRITING PROJECTS

- Brainstorm ideas before writing.
- Make lists of your ideas.
- Put numbers next to the ideas to determine the order in which you want to write about them.
- Group your ideas into paragraphs.
- Skip lines in your rough draft.
- Have a partner read your work and give you feedback on the meaning and language structure.
- Set it aside and reread it at least once before doing a final draft. Double-check verb endings, adjective agreements, and accents.
- Read it once again to check that you said what you meant to say.
- Be sure to have a title and any necessary illustrations or bibliography.

Did You Get It? *Presentación de vocabulario*

 ¡AVANZA! **Goal:** Learn words to talk about technology.

Technology

- Technology is part of our everyday lives. Read the following words you can use to talk about computers.

Parts of a computer	**la pantalla** *(screen)* **el ratón** *(mouse)* **el teclado** *(keyboard)*
The Internet	**estar en línea** *(to be online)* **conectarse a Internet** *(to connect to the Internet)* **hacer clic en** *(to click on)* **navegar por Internet** *(to surf the Internet)* **el sitio Web** *(Web site)* **el icono** *(icon)*
Communicating online	**la dirección electrónica** *(e–mail address)* **correos electrónicos** *(e–mails)* **el mensajero instantáneo** *(instant messaging)* **mandar** *(to send)*

- Read the paragraph below to learn more technology terms.

What I like to do most is to take photos **(tomar fotos)** with my digital camera **(cámara digital)**. Last week **(la semana pasada)** my friends and I went to the beach, and I took a lot of pictures. The day before yesterday **(anteayer)** I uploaded the pictures onto my computer. Today I'm going to burn a CD **(quemar un disco compacto)**. Finally **(por fin)**, I can share the pictures with my friends!

Did You Get It? *Práctica de vocabulario*

UNIDAD 7 Lección 1

Reteaching and Practice

> ⮞ **¡AVANZA!** **Goal:** Learn words to talk about technology.

❶ Match the following Spanish words with their English translations.

1. el icono _____ digital camera
2. la dirección electrónica _____ icon
3. el teclado _____ Website
4. el mensajero instantáneo _____ mouse
5. la pantalla _____ keyboard
6. el sitio Web _____ e–mail address
7. el ratón _____ instant messaging
8. la cámara digital _____ screen

❷ Write the correct translation.

1. to burn a CD _____
2. to connect to the Internet _____
3. to click on _____
4. to surf the Internet _____
5. to take photos _____
6. to send _____
7. to be online _____

❸ Use the words and phrases in the box to complete the e–mail.

| por fin | semana pasada | anteayer | conectarse a Internet | dirección electrónica |

A: Ana Luisa

De: Andrés

Hola, Ana Luisa,

¿Cómo estás? El sábado de la _____ mis padres me compraron una
computadora. _____ tengo una _____ . Ahora
puedo _____ para escribirles correos electrónicos a todos mis amigos.
_____ recibí mi primer correo electrónico. ¿Me vas a escribir? ¡Espero
que sí!

Andrés

4 Complete each sentence.

1. Tomo fotos con mi _____ .

2. Uso _____ para hacer clic en los iconos.

3. Puedo hablar con mis amigos con _____ .

4. Antes de navegar por Internet, necesito _____ .

5. Quiero mandarte un correo electrónico. ¿Me das tu _____ ?

6. Me gusta la _____ grande porque puedo ver mejor.

7. Elena me _____ un mensaje instantáneo.

8. Me gusta esa música. ¿Me puedes _____ ?

9. Uso las dos manos cuando escribo en _____ .

10. Me gusta ese _____ porque tiene mucha información.

5 Choose a logical response from the box for each statement. Use each response only once.

Le pide su dirección electrónica	**Va a usar el mensajero instantáneo.**
Hace clic en el icono.	**Va a leer su correo electrónico.**
Busca su cámara digital.	**Navega por Internet.**

1. Elena quiere tomar fotos. _____

2. José quiere información sobre Abraham Lincoln. _____

3. Ana quiere mandar un correo electrónico a Jorge. _____

4. Lupe quiere hablar con Isabel ahora. _____

5. Isabel quiere abrir un documento. _____

6. Rolando quiere saber si su amigo le escribió. _____

6 Write three sentences explaining three things you can do on the Internet.

1. _____

2. _____

3. _____

Did You Get It? *Presentación de gramática*

 Goal: Learn about the preterite tense of **-er** and **-ir** verbs.

The Preterite Form of Regular -er and -ir Verbs

- Remember that the preterite is a tense used to express an action completed at a definite time in the past. In English, regular verbs in the past tense end in *-ed*. Study the different forms of **comer** and **escribir** in the preterite.

comer *(to eat)*		**escribir** *(to write)*	
comí	**comimos**	**escribí**	**escribimos**
comiste	**comisteis**	**escribiste**	**escribisteis**
comió	**comieron**	**escribió**	**escribieron**

EXPLANATION: Regular **-er** and **-ir** verbs follow a pattern similar to regular **-ar** verbs in the *preterite*. Notice that the **yo** and the **él/ella/usted** forms have accents. Also, the **nosotros(as)** preterite form of **-ir** verbs is the same as the present tense. Use context clues in these sentences to determine when the activity occurred. For example:

Present

Siempre **escribimos** muchos correos electrónicos.

*(We always **write** a lot of e–mails.)*

Preterite

Ayer **escribimos** muchos correos electrónicos.

*(Yesterday **we wrote** a lot of e–mails.)*

Did You Get It? *Práctica de gramática*

¡AVANZA!   **Goal:**   Learn about the preterite tense of **-er** and **-ir** verbs.

❶ Write the correct subject pronoun for each preterite form.

1. escribieron _____
2. volviste _____
3. recibí _____
4. abrimos _____
5. comió _____

6. bebí _____
7. vendieron _____
8. viviste _____
9. escribimos _____
10. corrieron _____

❷ Complete each sentence with the correct form of the verb in parentheses.

1. Mi hermana _____ en Brasil. **(vivir)**
2. Tomás _____ su televisor. **(vender)**
3. Nosotros _____ correos electrónicos la semana pasada. **(escribir)**
4. Juan _____ la puerta. **(abrir)**
5. Ustedes no _____ mi correo electrónico. **(recibir)**
6. Él _____ mucho pastel. **(comer)**
7. Ustedes no _____ el jugo de naranja. **(beber)**
8. Cristina _____ a casa temprano. **(volver)**
9. Yo _____ en el parque. **(correr)**
10. Tú _____ todos los animales en el zoológico. **(ver)**

❸ Change the following sentences from the present to the preterite.

1. Tú pides la cuenta. _____
2. Ustedes comen el almuerzo. _____
3. Yo bebo un refresco. _____
4. Mi hermana y yo volvemos tarde. _____
5. Ustedes corren en el parque. _____
6. Él aprende español. _____
7. Isabel escribe un correo electrónico. _____
8. Nosotros vivimos en la ciudad. _____
9. ¿Recibes muchos correos electrónicos? _____
10. Suben la escalera. _____

❹ Use the subjects and phrases given to write complete sentences in the preterite. Follow the model.

Model: yo / escribir un correo electrónico ayer

Yo escribí un correo electrónico ayer.

1. Elena / vender la pantalla anteayer

_____

2. mis padres / salir a las siete de la mañana

_____

3. Tomás y yo / volver la semana pasada

_____

4. mi tía / recibir mi correo electrónico

_____

5. los estudiantes / correr en el parque después de las clases

_____

❺ Translate the sentences into Spanish.

1. Jorge and Pedro drank the water. _____

2. I sold some CDs yesterday. _____

3. She received good grades. _____

4. They left the pool at two o'clock. _____

5. You returned to class late. _____

6. My parents sold the house last week. _____

7. They lost the digital camera. _____

8. Alex and Lola sent me two e–mails. _____

9. I ate pizza at school. _____

10. Ana understood all the soccer rules. _____

❻ Write five sentences describing what you and the following people did yesterday.

1. yo _____

2. mis padres _____

3. mis hermanos _____

4. mis amigos y yo _____

5. mi mejor amigo(a) _____

Did You Get It? *Presentación de gramática*

 ¡AVANZA! **Goal:** Learn how to use affirmative and negative words.

Affirmative and Negative Words

- Use an affirmative or a negative word when you want to talk about an indefinite or negative situation. Study the list of affirmative and negative words below.

Affirmative Words		*Negative Words*	
algo	*(something)*	**nada**	*(nothing)*
alguien	*(someone)*	**nadie**	*(no one)*
algún / alguno(a)	*(some / any)*	**ningún / ninguno(a)**	*(none / not any)*
o… o	*(either…or)*	**ni… ni**	*(neither…nor)*
siempre	*(always)*	**nunca**	*(never)*
también	*(also)*	**tampoco**	*(neither, not either)*

- Read the sentences below, paying attention to the boldfaced words.

¿Conoces **algún** chico uruguayo?

*(Do you know **any** Uruguayan boys?)*

No conozco a **ningún** chico uruguayo.

*(I do not know **any** Uruguayan boys.)*

EXPLANATION: **Alguno(a)** and **ninguno(a)** match the gender of the noun they replace or modify. They have different forms when used before masculine singular nouns: **alguno** becomes **algún** and **ninguno** becomes **ningún**.

- Study the sentences below, paying attention to the boldfaced words.

No quiero **nada**.

*(**I** do **not** want **anything**.)*

No me gusta **ninguna** computadora.

*(**I** do **not** like **any** computers.)*

EXPLANATION: A double negative is required in Spanish when **no** precedes the verb.

- Read these sentences, paying attention to the boldfaced words.

Yo **nunca** uso una cámara digital.

*(**I** **never** use a digital camera.)*

Nadie quiere navegar por Internet.

*(**No one** wants to surf the Web.)*

EXPLANATION: If the negative word comes before the verb, there is no need to use **no**.

Did You Get It? *Práctica de gramática*

¡AVANZA!　　**Goal:**　Learn how to use affirmative and negative words.

❶ Circle the correct affirmative or negative word to complete each sentence.

　1. No quiero ver _____ película de horror. **(alguna, ninguna)**

　2. Mi madre quiere comprar _____ en el centro comercial. **(algo, nada)**

　3. No conocemos a _____ en la clase. **(nadie, alguien)**

　4. ¿Quieres practicar _____ deporte? **(algún, ningún)**

　5. No conoce _____ sitio Web interesante. **(ningún, algún)**

　6. ¿Quieres ver _____ película cómica? **(ninguna, alguna)**

　7. ¿Te gusta _____ cámara digital? **(ninguna, alguna)**

　8. Por el momento, no queremos _____. **(nada, algo)**

　9. No viene _____ al cine conmigo. **(alguien, nadie)**

　10. ¿Quieres _____ libros para leer? **(ningún, algunos)**

❷ Rewrite the following sentences, using a single negative. Follow the model.

　Modelo:　No preparo nunca la comida. *Nunca preparo la comida.*

　1. No hablo nunca en la clase. _____

　2. No me escribe nadie. _____

　3. No salen nunca con Paco. _____

　4. No me ve nadie. _____

　5. No manda nunca correos electrónicos. _____

　6. No me compra nunca un regalo. _____

　7. No viene nadie mañana. _____

　8. No como galletas nunca. _____

Nombre _____ Clase _____ Fecha _____

❸ Answer the following questions with a negative response. Follow the model.

Modelo: ¿Quieres algún postre? *No, no quiero ningún postre.*

1. ¿Va alguien a la fiesta contigo? _____

2. ¿Practicas algún deporte? _____

3. ¿Usas siempre la computadora? _____

4. ¿Estudias con alguien? _____

5. ¿Compras algo en la tienda de ropa? _____

6. ¿Estás escribiendo algún correo electrónico ahora? _____

_____

7. ¿Quieres comer algo? _____

❹ Answer the following questions with a negative response. Follow the model.

Modelo: ¿Quieres estudiar o escuchar música? *No quiero ni estudiar ni escuchar música.*

1. ¿Tocas el piano o la guitarra? _____

2. ¿Quieres comer pizza o papas fritas? _____

3. ¿Quieres ir al teatro o al cine? _____

4. ¿Quieres jugar al fútbol o al tenis? _____

5. ¿Escribes una carta o un correo electrónico? _____

6. ¿Vas a casa o a la escuela? _____

7. ¿Preparas el almuerzo o la cena? _____

8. ¿Lees el periódico o una novela? _____

❺ Complete the following conversation with the correct affirmative or negative words.

Linda: Hola, Alicia. ¿Adónde vas hoy?

Alicia: Voy al centro comercial.

Linda: ¿Quién va contigo?

Alicia: _____ viene conmigo. ¿Quieres venir tú?

Linda: Sí. Quiero comprar _____ pantalones.

Alicia: Yo no quiero comprar _____ pantalón pero quiero comprar _____ disco compacto.

Linda: Ay, pero tú siempre compras discos compactos.

Alicia: No es verdad, Linda. ¡Yo _____ compro discos compactos!

Linda: Entonces, ¿cómo es *(how come)* que tienes más de cuatrocientos?

✿ ¿Recuerdas?

Level 1 p. 360
Level 1B p. 171

Affirmative tú Commands

• Review the formation of regular affirmative **tú** commands.

Infinitive	Present Tense	Affirmative tú command
caminar *(to walk)*	**Él camina.** *(He walks.)*	**¡Camina rápido!** *(Walk quickly!)*
correr *(to run)*	**Él corre.** *(He runs.)*	**¡Corre rápido!** *(Run quickly!)*
escribir *(to write)*	**Él escribe.** *(He writes.)*	**¡Escribe rápido!** *(Write quickly!)*

• Review these verbs that have irregular affirmative **tú** commands.

Infinitive	decir *(to say)*	hacer *(to make, to do)*	ir *(to go)*	poner *(to put)*	salir *(to leave)*	ser *(to be)*	tener *(to have)*	venir *(to come)*
Affirmative **tú** command	**di**	**haz**	**ve**	**pon**	**sal**	**sé**	**ten**	**ven**

• Remember to *attach* a direct object pronoun to the end of the command and to add an accent to commands of two or more syllables. For example:

¡Abre **la ventana**! ⟶ ¡Ábre**la**!   ¡Come **el pollo**! ⟶ ¡Cóme**lo**!

*(Open **the window**!)*   *(Open **it**!)*   *(Eat **the chicken**!)*   *(Eat **it**!)*

Práctica

❶ Answer the following questions, using affirmative **tú** commands. Follow the model.

   Modelo: ¿Uso el ratón?   *Sí, úsalo.*

  1. ¿Mando el correo electrónico? _____

  2. ¿Leo el mensaje? _____

  3. ¿Miro la pantalla? _____

  4. ¿Leo las instrucciones? _____

  5. ¿Digo el secreto? _____

❷ Translate each set of affirmative **tú** commands into Spanish.

  1. Write the e–mail! _____ Write it! _____

  2. Burn the CDs! _____ Burn them! _____

  3. Look at the screen! _____ Look at it! _____

  4. Open the book! _____ Open it! _____

  5. Take the photos! _____ Take them! _____

♲ ¿Recuerdas?

Telling time

• Review the times in Spanish below.

4:00	11:30	1:00
Son las cuatro.	Son las once y media.	Es la una.
5:15	11:40	7:10
Son las cinco y cuarto.	Son las doce menos veinte.	Son las siete y diez.

Foods and beverages

• Review the following foods (comidas) and drinks (bebidas).

las manzanas *(apples)*	las bananas *(bananas)*	las uvas *(grapes)*
el cereal *(cereal)*	el pan *(bread)*	el yogur *(yogurt)*
los huevos *(eggs)*	el café *(coffee)*	la hamburguesa *(hamburger)*
el jugo de naranja *(orange juice)*	la leche *(milk)*	la sopa *(soup)*

Práctica

Translate the following sentences into Spanish. The first one is done for you.

1. Andrea ate cereal at 8:00.   *Andrea comió cereal a las ocho.*

2. We ate an apple at 10:30.

   _____

3. You all (ustedes) ate eggs at ten o'clock.

   _____

4. The boys ate hamburgers at 6:10.

   _____

5. You (tú) drank a glass of orange juice at 9:45.

   _____

6. You (usted) drank a coffee at 2:20.

   _____

7. Alicia and I ate some grapes at 8:30.

   _____

♻ ¿Recuerdas?

Level 1 p. 368
Level 1B p. 180

Preterite of regular -ar verbs

• Review the preterite conjugation of regular **-ar** verbs below.

yo	**-é**	nosotros(as)	**-amos**
tú	**-aste**	vosotros(as)	**-asteis**
él/ella/usted	**-ó**	ellos(as)/ustedes	**-aron**

• Remember that regular **-ar** verbs ending in **-car, -gar,** or **-zar** have a spelling change in the **yo** form of the preterite. Review these changes below.

buscar   → yo busqué

jugar   → yo jugué

almorzar → yo almorcé

Práctica

❶ Complete each sentence with the correct preterite form of a verb from the box. Use each verb only once.

> **almorzar jugar nadar comprar estudiar escuchar patinar ganar bailar caminar**

  1. Nina _____ en el mar.

  2. Yo _____ en un restaurante la semana pasada.

  3. Nosotros _____ al básquetbol en la cancha.

  4. Juan y María _____ en la playa.

  5. Lina _____ un vestido nuevo.

  6. Enrique y yo _____ música ayer.

  7. Ustedes _____ mucho en la fiesta.

  8. Tú _____ el partido.

  9. Yo _____ en línea anteayer.

  10. ¿ _____ tú anoche para el examen?

❷ Use regular **-ar** verbs you know to write at least two things you and the following people did yesterday.

  1. Yo _____

  2. Mi maestro(a) de español _____

  3. Mis amigos y yo _____

Did You Get It? *Presentación de vocabulario*

> **¡AVANZA!**   **Goal:**   Learn terms for talking on the phone and making plans.

Making Plans

• Making plans with friends is fun. Read the following terms that will help you learn how to make plans in Spanish.

Making the call:	**llamar** *(to call)*
	el teléfono celular *(cellular phone)*
	¿Aló? *(Hello?)*
	¿Puedo hablar con... ? *(May I speak with...?)*
The invitation:	**¿Te gustaría... ?** *(Would you like...?)*
	Me gustaría... *(I would like...)*
	¿Quieres acompañarme a... ? *(Would you like to come with me to...?)*
	Te invito. *(I'll treat you. / I invite you.)*
	el fin de semana *(weekend)*
Where to go:	**el acuario** *(aquarium)*
	la feria *(fair)*
	el museo *(museum)*
	el zoológico *(zoo)*
The response:	**¡Claro que sí!** *(Of course!)*
	¡Qué lástima! *(What a shame!)*

• Read the paragraph to learn words you can use to talk about one of the most fun places to go.

So, you've decided to go to the amusement park **(el parque de diversiones)**. How fun! **(¡Qué divertido!)**. If you don't like heights, you probably won't want to ride **(subir a)** the Ferris wheel **(la vuelta al mundo)**. How scary! **(¡Qué miedo!)** But who can resist the excitement of the bumper cars **(los autitos chocadores)** and the sudden dips of the roller coaster **(la montaña rusa)**! So, what are you waiting for—buy plenty of tickets **(boletos)** and enjoy the rides!

Did You Get It? *Práctica de vocabulario*

¡AVANZA! **Goal:** Learn terms for talking on the phone and making plans.

1 Identify these items found at the amusement park.

1. _____

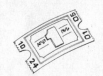

2. _____

3. _____

4. _____

2 State where the people are going based on what they want to do. The first one is done for you.

1. Juan quiere ver los elefantes. *Va al zoológico.*

2. Lucía quiere ver los peces (*fish*). _____

3. Antonio y José quieren subir a la montaña rusa. _____

4. María quiere ver cuadros. _____

3 Complete the following telephone conversation using the terms provided.

tengo miedo	aló	acompañarme
con	subir a	llamar
te gustaría	teléfono celular	fin de semana

Elena: ¿ _____ ? ¿Puedo hablar con Miguel?

Miguel: Hola, Elena. Soy yo, Miguel.

Elena: Hola, Miguel. ¿Quieres _____ al acuario este _____ ?

Miguel: ¡Qué lastima! No puedo. ¿ _____ ir _____ mi familia al parque de diversiones?

Elena: Me gustaría ir pero _____ de la montaña rusa.

Miguel: ¿Te gusta _____ a los autitos chocadores?

Elena: ¡Claro que sí!

Miguel: ¡Perfecto! Te voy a _____ mañana en la mañana.

Elena: Llámame al _____ . Hasta mañana.

4 Choose the most logical response.

1. Voy al parque de diversiones.

   ¿Aló?   ¡Qué divertido!   ¿Puedo hablar con...?

2. ¿Quieres acompañarme al acuario?

   ¿Puedo hablar contigo?   ¿Te gustaría ir?   ¡Claro que sí!

3. Quiero subir a la montaña rusa.

   ¡Qué miedo!   ¿Puedo hablar contigo?   ¡Qué lástima!

4. No puedo ir al museo contigo.

   ¿Aló?   ¡Qué lástima!   Te invito.

5. ¿Puedo hablar con Elena?

   ¡Qué miedo!   Me gustaría...   Sí, soy yo.

6. ¿Aló?

   ¿Puedo hablar con Álex?   Me gustaría ir.   ¡Qué lástima!

7. No puedo ir porque no tengo dinero.

   ¡Claro que sí!   ¿Aló?   Yo te invito.

8. ¿Vas a la feria mañana?

   Sí. ¿Quieres acompañarme?   ¡Qué miedo!   Te invito.

5 Write three sentences explaining where you like to go for fun, with whom you go, and what you do there. Follow the model.

Modelo: *Me gusta ir al parque de diversiones.*

Voy con mis amigos o con mi familia.

Subo a la montaña rusa y a la vuelta al mundo.

1. _____

2. _____

3. _____

Did You Get It? *Presentación de gramática*

 Goal: Learn about the irregular preterite form of **ir** *(to go)*, **ser** *(to be)*, and **hacer** *(to do, to make)*.

Preterite of ir and ser

• Review the following sentences, paying close attention to the boldfaced words.

Fui al parque de diversiones.
*(I **went** to the amusement park.)*

Fue un día divertido.
*(It **was** a very fun day.)*

Fuimos al museo.
*(We **went** to the museum.)*

Fue muy interesante.
*(It **was** very interesting.)*

EXPLANATION: The verbs **ir** *(to go)* and **ser** *(to be)* are irregular in the preterite. They are also exactly the same. You can use context clues to help you know which verb is being used. Use the chart below as a quick reference for the different forms of **ir** and **ser** in the preterite.

ir *(to go)* / ser *(to be)*	
fui	fuimos
fuiste	fuisteis
fue	fueron

Preterite of hacer

• Read the following sentences, paying close attention to the boldfaced words.

Hice un pastel.
*(I **made** a cake.)*

Hicieron la tarea.
*(They **did** homework.)*

EXPLANATION: The verb **hacer** is also irregular in the preterite. Like **ir** and **ser**, the preterite forms of **hacer** have no accents. Also, notice that the **c** becomes **z** before **o**. Study the chart below and use it as a quick reference for the different forms of **hacer**.

hacer *(to do, to make)*	
hice	hicimos
hiciste	hicisteis
hizo	hicieron

UNIDAD 7 Lección 2

Reteaching and Practice

Nombre _____ Clase _____ Fecha _____

Did You Get It? *Práctica de gramática*

 ¡AVANZA! **Goal:** Learn about the irregular preterite form of **ir** *(to go)*, **ser** *(to be)*, and **hacer** *(to do, to make)*.

1 Write the correct preterite form with the subject given.

1. yo **(ir)** _____
2. ellos **(hacer)** _____
3. Juan y yo **(ser)** _____
4. los estudiantes **(hacer)** _____
5. tú **(ir)** _____
6. Elena **(ser)** _____
7. vosotros **(hacer)** _____
8. yo **(hacer)** _____

2 Complete the following sentences with the preterite of each verb.

1. Luis _____ a la feria. **(ir)**
2. Nosotros _____ la tarea. **(hacer)**
3. El día _____ muy divertido. **(ser)**
4. Ella _____ al museo. **(ir)**
5. Ana _____ la cama. **(hacer)**
6. Ellos _____ al zoológico. **(ir)**
7. ¿ _____ aburrido el museo? **(ser)**
8. Yo _____ la tarea. **(hacer)**

3 Answer the following questions in complete sentences. Follow the model.

Modelo: ¿Fuiste al museo el sábado pasado?

Sí, fui al museo el sábado pasado. or *No, no fui al museo el sábado pasado.*

1. ¿Hiciste la cama esta mañana?

_____

2. ¿Adónde fueron tú y tus amigos el fin de semana pasado?

_____

3. ¿Fue un día interesante hoy?

_____

4. ¿Hiciste la tarea de español anoche?

_____

4 Translate the following sentences into Spanish.

1. José went to the museum. _____

2. What did she do yesterday? _____

3. The math class was interesting. _____

4. I made the bed. _____

5. They went to the book fair. _____

6. We made the salad. _____

7. We did the homework. _____

8. The homework was easy. _____

9. The day was fun. _____

10. Did you go to the museum? _____

5 Write four or five sentences describing what you did last Saturday. Follow the model.

Modelo: *El sábado pasado, mis amigos y yo fuimos al museo. Después, fuimos al cine. Por la noche, hice la comida para todos. ¡Fue un día divertido!*

_____

_____

_____

_____

Did You Get It? *Presentación de gramática*

 Goal: Use pronouns after prepositions like **a**, **con**, **de**, and **para**.

Pronouns After Prepositions

- Who's the ticket for? Read the sentences below, paying attention to the boldfaced words.

Es **para mí**.	*(It's for me.)*	Es **para nosotros(as)**.	*(It's for us.)*
Es **para ti**.	*(It's for you.)*	Es **para vosotros(as)**.	*(It's for you.)*
Es **para él/ella/usted**.	*(It's for him/her/you.)*	Es **para ellos(as)/ustedes**.	*(It's for them/you.)*

EXPLANATION: Pronouns that follow prepositions such as **para** *(for)*, **cerca de** *(near)*, **detrás de** *(behind)*, and **para** *(for)* are the same as the subject pronouns in all forms except **mí** (**yo**) and **ti** (**tú**). Review the chart below and use it as a quick reference for pronouns that follow prepositions in Spanish.

Pronouns After Prepositions	
mí	nosotros(as)
ti	vosotros(as)
él, ella, usted	ellos(as), ustedes

Conmigo / Contigo

- Read the sentences below, paying attention to the highlighted words.

¿Voy al acuario *con***tigo**?　　　*(Am I going to the aquarium **with you**?)*

¡Claro que sí! Vienes *con***migo**.　*(Of course! You are coming **with me**.)*

EXPLANATION: When **mí** and **ti** are used after the preposition **con**, they combine with **con** to form the words **conmigo** and **contigo**.

Did You Get It? *Práctica de gramática*

¡AVANZA!	**Goal:** Use pronouns after prepositions like **a**, **con**, **de**, and **para**.

1 Answer the question using a pronoun in Spanish. The first one is done for you.

Es para...

1. Julio *él* _____
2. the girls _____
3. me _____
4. my grandmother _____

5. Elena and Luis _____
6. Juan and me _____
7. you, singular _____
8. you, plural _____

2 Complete each sentence using the words provided.

usted	mí	conmigo	nosotros	contigo	ti

1. Emilio, la montaña rusa está enfrente de _____ .
2. Voy al museo. ¿Quieres ir _____ ?
3. Dicen que está delante de _____ , pero yo no lo veo.
4. Señora Pérez, el regalo es para _____ .
5. ¿Vas a la feria? ¿Puedo ir _____ ?
6. Ana y yo vamos al zoológico. A _____ nos gustan los animales.

3 Describe where each person is in relation to the attraction. The first one is done for you.

1.

2.

3.

4.

1. la montaña rusa / los chicos

   La montaña rusa está cerca de ellos. _____

2. la vuelta al mundo / las chicas

   _____

3. el acuario / el señor Hernández

   _____

4. el zoológico / yo

   _____

4 Complete the telephone conversation with the correct pronouns.

Ángela: Hola, Señor Ávila. Soy Ángela. ¿Está Juan en casa?

Señor Ávila: Sí, Ángela. Está haciendo la tarea.

Ángela: Bueno, ¿puedo hablar con *(him)* _____ ?

Señor Ávila: ¡Claro que sí! Un momento.

Juan: Hola, Ángela. ¿Cómo estás?

Ángela: Bien, Juan. ¿Te gustaría ir al museo *(with me)* _____ el sábado?

Juan: Me gustaría ir *(with you)* _____ pero no puedo. Voy al acauario con Jorge.

Ángela: ¿Y no puedes ir con *(him)* _____ el domingo.

Juan: No, porque él va al parque de diversiones con Luisa el domingo.

Ángela: ¿Y Jorge no puede ir con *(her)* _____ el lunes?

Juan: No, porque ella va al acuario con Isabel y Natalia el lunes.

Ángela: ¿Y Luisa no puede ir con *(them)* _____ el martes?

Juan: No, porque ellas van con *(us)* _____ a la feria de libros el martes.

Ángela: Ah, sí. Tienes razón. Bueno, entonces, ¡hasta el martes!

5 Answer the questions, using pronouns in your response.

1. ¿Te gustaría ir al parque de diversiones con tus amigos?

_____

2. ¿Qué prefieres hacer con tu mejor amigo: subir a la montaña rusa o a la vuelta al mundo?

_____

3. ¿Quieres ir de vacaciones con tus padres?

_____

4. ¿Qué dices cuando hay un regalo para ti?

_____

6 Write a telephone conversation asking a friend to go somewhere with you.

_____

_____

_____

_____

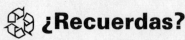 **¿Recuerdas?**

Level 1 p. 384
Level 1B p. 199

Noun-adjective agreement

- Remember that in Spanish, adjectives must agree in gender and number with the nouns they describe. Study the following sentences.

—El chico es alto.	*(The boy is tall.)*
—Sí. ¡Qué alto!	*(Yes. How tall!)*
—La chica es guapa.	*(The girl is pretty.)*
—Sí. ¡Qué guapa!	*(Yes. How pretty!)*
—Los chicos son cómicos.	*(The boys are funny.)*
—Sí. ¡Qué cómicos!	*(Yes. How funny!)*
—Las chicas son atléticas.	*(The girls are athletic.)*
—Sí. ¡Qué atléticas!	*(Yes. How athletic!)*
—Los chicos son interesantes.	*(The boys are interesting.)*
—Sí. ¡Qué interesantes!	*(Yes. How interesting!)*
—Las chicas son inteligentes.	*(The girls are intelligent.)*
—Sí. ¡Qué inteligentes!	*(Yes. How intelligent!)*

Práctica

1 Write the correct adjective for each noun.

1. el chico *(handsome)* _____

2. los gatos *(small)* _____

3. la maestra *(intelligent)* _____

4. la chica *(pretty)* _____

5. las estudiantes *(creative)* _____

2 Write your reaction to each of the following. Make sure the adjective agrees with the noun. The first one is done for you.

divertido	peligroso	interesante	aburrido	cómico

1. amusement parks *¡Qué divertidos!*

2. the roller coaster _____

3. history museums _____

4. your Spanish class _____

5. your best friends _____

¿Recuerdas?

Places around town

- Review the names of several places (**lugares**) below.

el café	*(café)*	**el centro**	*(center, downtown)*
el cine	*(movie theater, the movies)*	**el concierto**	*(concert)*
el parque	*(park)*	**el restaurante**	*(restaurant)*
el teatro	*(theater)*	**la calle**	*(street)*

Práctica

1 Match the following.

1. el parque   _____ movie theater
2. el café   _____ street
3. el cine   _____ restaurant
4. el centro   _____ concert
5. la calle   _____ café
6. el concierto   _____ downtown
7. el teatro   _____ park
8. el restaurante   _____ theater

2 Complete the following sentences.

1. Voy al _____ para hacer las compras.
2. Elena va al _____ con su perro.
3. ¿Quieres ir al _____ a ver una película?
4. Vamos al _____ para comer un pastel.
5. Voy al _____ para ver una ópera.
6. Isabel y Luis van al _____ para cenar.
7. Ellas van al _____ para escuchar música.
8. Camino por la _____ .

¿Recuerdas?

Stem–changing verbs: e → i

- Review the conjugations of these two present tense verbs whose stems change from **e** to **i**.

pedir *(to ask)*			
yo	**pido**	nosotros(as)	**pedimos**
tú	**pides**	vosotros(as)	**pedís**
él/ella/usted	**pide**	ellos(as)/ustedes	**piden**

servir *(to serve)*			
yo	**sirvo**	nosotros(as)	**servimos**
tú	**sirves**	vosotros(as)	**servís**
él/ella/usted	**sirve**	ellos(as)/ustedes	**sirven**

EXPLANATION: Present tense verbs that have stems that change from **e** to **i** change in all forms except **nosotros(as)** and **vosotros(as)**.

Práctica

Tell what each person orders. The first one is done for you.

1. Mi padre / una ensalada
   Mi padre pide una ensalada.

6. Yo / las verduras
_____

2. Mis amigos / el pollo
_____

7. María / un café
_____

3. Tú / un café
_____

8. Ustedes / el arroz
_____

4. Mis abuelos / el pescado
_____

9. Raúl / la carne
_____

5. Ángela y yo / un pastel
_____

10. Nosotros / las patatas
_____

Did You Get It? Answer Key

PRÁCTICA DE VOCABULARIO

TECHNOLOGY, pp. 2–3

❶

1. icon
2. e-mail address
3. keyboard
4. instant messaging
5. screen
6. Web site
7. mouse
8. digital camera

❷

1. quemar un dísco compacto
2. conectarse al Internet
3. hacer chic en
4. navegar por Internet
5. tomar fotos
6. mandar
7. estar en línea

❸ Hola, Ana Luisa,

¿Cómo estás? El sábado de la **semana pasada** mis padres me compraron una computadora. **Por fin** tengo una **dirección electrónica**. Ahora puedo **conectarme a Internet** para escribirles correos electrónicos a todos mis amigos. **Anteayer**, recibí mi primer correo electrónico. ¿Me vas a escribir? ¡Espero que sí!

Andrés

❹

1. cámara digital
2. el ratón
3. el mensajero instantáneo
4. estar en línea / conectarme a Internet
5. dirección electrónica
6. pantalla
7. manda
8. quemar un disco compacto
9. el teclado
10. sitio Web

❺

1. Busca su cámara digital.
2. Navega por Internet.
3. Le pide su dirección electrónica.
4. Va a usar el mensajero instantáneo.
5. Hace clic en el icono.
6. Va a leer su correo electrónico.

❻ Answers will vary.

PRÁCTICA DE GRAMÁTICA

THE PRETERITE FORM OF REGULAR –**ER** AND –**IR** VERBS, pp. 5–6

❶

1. usteded/ellos(as)
2. tú
3. yo
4. nosotros(as)
5. él/ella/usted
6. yo
7. ellos(as)/ustedes
8. tú
9. nosotros(as)
10. usteded/ellos(as)

❷

1. vivió
2. vendió
3. escribimos
4. abrió
5. recibieron
6. comió
7. bebieron
8. volvió
9. corrí
10. viste

❸

1. Tú pediste la cuenta.
2. Ustedes comieron el almuerzo.
3. Yo bebí un refresco.
4. Mi hermana y yo volvimos tarde.
5. Ustedes corrieron en el parque.
6. Él aprendió español.
7. Isabel escribió un correo electrónico.
8. Nosotros vivimos en la ciudad.
9. ¿Recibiste muchos correos electrónicos?
10. Subieron la escalera.

Did You Get It? Answer Key

④

1. Elena vendió la pantalla anteayer.
2. Mis padres salieron a las siete de la mañana.
3. Tomás y yo volvimos la semana pasada.
4. Mi tía recibió mi correo electrónico.
5. Los estudiantes corrieron en el parque después de las clases.

⑤

1. Jorge y Pedro bebieron el agua.
2. Ayer vendí unos discos compactos.
3. Ella recibió buenas notas.
4. Ellos salieron de la piscina a las dos.
5. Tú volviste tarde a clase.
6. Mis padres vendieron la casa la semana pasada.
7. Perdieron la cámara digital.
8. Álex y Lola me mandaron dos correos electrónicos.
9. Comí pizza en la escuela.
10. Ana comprendió todas las reglas del fútbol.

⑥ Answers will vary.

PRÁCTICA DE GRAMÁTICA

AFFIRMATIVE AND NEGATIVE WORDS, pp. 8–9

①

1. ninguna	2. algo
3. nadie	4. algún
5. ningún	6. alguna
7. alguna	8. nada
9. nadie	10. algunos

②

1. Nunca hablo en la clase.
2. Nadie me escribe.
3. Nunca salen con Paco.
4. Nadie me ve.
5. Nunca manda correos electrónicos.
6. Nunca me compra un regalo.
7. Nadie viene mañana.
8. Nunca como galletas.

③

1. No, no va nadie a la fiesta conmigo.
2. No, no practico ningún deporte.
3. No, no uso nunca la computadora.
4. No, no estudio con nadie.
5. No, no compro nada en la tienda de ropa.
6. No, no estoy escribiendo ningún correo electrónico ahora.
7. No, no quiero comer nada.

④

1. No toco ni el piano ni la guitarra.
2. No quiero comer ni pizza ni papas fritas.
3. No quiero ir ni al teatro ni al cine.
4. No quiero jugar ni al fútbol ni al tenis.
5. No escribo ni una carta ni un correo electrónico.
6. No voy ni a casa ni a la escuela.
7. No preparo ni el almuerzo ni la cena.
8. No leo ni el periódico ni una novela.

Did You Get It? Answer Key

5

Linda: Hola, Alicia. ¿Adónde vas hoy?

Alicia: Voy al centro comercial.

Linda: ¿Quién va contigo?

Alicia: **Nadie** viene conmigo. ¿Quieres venir tú?

Linda: Sí. Quiero comprar **algunos** pantalones.

Alicia: Yo no quiero comprar **ningún** pantalón pero quiero comprar **algún** disco compacto.

Linda: Ay, pero tú siempre compras discos compactos.

Alicia: No es verdad, Linda. ¡Yo **nunca** compro discos compactos!

Linda: Entonces, ¿cómo es *(how come)* que tienes más de cuatrocientos?

 ¿RECUERDAS?

AFFIRMATIVE **TÚ** COMMANDS, p. 10

Práctica

1

1. Sí, mándalo.
2. Sí, léelo.
3. Sí, mírala.
4. Sí, léelas.
5. Sí, dilo.

2

1. ¡Escribe el correo electrónico! ¡Escríbelo!
2. ¡Quema los discos compactos! ¡Quémalos!
3. ¡Mira la pantalla! ¡Mírala!
4. ¡Abre el libro! ¡Ábrelo!
5. ¡Toma las fotos! ¡Tómalas!

 ¿RECUERDAS?

TELLING TIME, p. 11

Práctica

1. *Andrea comió cereal a las ocho.*
2. Nosotros comimos una manzana a las diez y media.
3. Ustedes comieron huevos a las diez.
4. Los chicos comieron hamburguesas a las seis y diez.
5. Tú bebiste un jugo de naranja a las diez menos cuarto.
6. Usted bebió un café a las dos y veinte.
7. Alicia y yo comimos unas uvas a las ocho y media.

 ¿RECUERDAS?

PRETERITE OF REGULAR VERBS, p. 12

Práctica

1

1. nadó
2. almorcé
3. jugamos
4. caminaron
5. compró
6. escuchamos
7. bailaron
8. ganaste
9. patiné
10. Estudiaste

2 Answers will vary.

Did You Get It? Answer Key

PRÁCTICA DE VOCABULARIO

MAKING PLANS, pp. 14–15

❶

1. la vuelta al mundo
2. el boleto
3. los autitos chocadores
4. la montaña rusa

❷

1. *Va al zoológico.*
2. Va al acuario.
3. Van al parque de diversiones.
4. Va al museo.

❸

Elena: ¿Aló? ¿Puedo hablar con Miguel?

Miguel: Hola, Elena. Soy yo, Miguel.

Elena: Hola, Miguel. ¿Quieres **acompañarme** al acuario este **fin de semana**?

Miguel: ¡Qué lastima! No puedo. ¿**Te gustaría** ir **con** mi familia al parque de diversiones?

Elena: Me gustaría ir, pero **tengo miedo** de la montaña rusa.

Miguel: ¿Te gusta **subir a** los autitos chocadores?

Elena: ¡Claro que sí!

Miguel: ¡Perfecto! Te voy a **llamar** mañana en la mañana.

Elena: Llámame al **teléfono celular**. Hasta mañana.

❹

1. ¡Qué divertido!
2. ¡Claro que sí!
3. ¡Qué miedo!
4. ¡Qué lastima!
5. Sí, soy yo.
6. ¿Puedo hablar con Álex?
7. Yo te invito.
8. Sí. ¿Quieres acompañarme?

❺ Answers will vary.

PRÁCTICA DE GRAMÁTICA

PRETERITE OF **IR** AND **SER**, pp. 17–18

❶

1. fui	2. hicieron	3. fuimos
4. hicieron	5. fuiste	6. fue
7. hicisteis	8. hice	

❷

1. fue	2. hicimos	3. fue
4. fue	5. hizo	6. fueron
7. Fue	8. hice	

❸ Answers will vary.

❹

1. José fue al museo.
2. ¿Qué hizo ella ayer?
3. La clase de matemáticas fue interesante.
4. Yo hice la cama.
5. Ellos fueron a la feria de libros.
6. Nosotros hicimos la ensalada.
7. Hicimos la tarea.
8. La tarea fue fácil.
9. El día fue divertido.
10. ¿Fuiste al museo?

❺ Answers will vary.

Did You Get It? Answer Key

PRÁCTICA DE GRAMÁTICA
PRONOUNS AFTER PREPOSITIONS, pp. 20–21

1

1. *él*
2. ellas
3. mí
4. ella
5. ellos
6. nosotros
7. ti / usted
8. vosotros(as) / ustedes

2

1. ti
2. conmigo
3. mí
4. usted
5. contigo
6. nosotros

3

1. *La montaña rusa está cerca de ellos.*
2. La vuelta al mundo está lejos de ellas.
3. El acuario está detrás de él.
4. El zoológico está delante de mí.

4

Ángela:	Hola, Señor Ávila. Soy Ángela. ¿Está Juan en casa?
Señor Ávila:	Sí, Ángela. Está haciendo la tarea.
Ángela:	Bueno, ¿puedo hablar con **él**?
Señor Ávila:	¡Claro que sí! Un momento.

Juan:	Hola, Ángela. ¿Cómo estás?
Ángela:	Bien, Juan. ¿Te gustaría ir al museo **conmigo** el sábado?
Juan:	Me gustaría ir **contigo**, pero no puedo. Voy al acuario con Jorge.
Ángela:	¿Y no puedes ir con **él** el domingo.
Juan:	No, porque él va al parque de diversiones con Luisa el domingo.
Ángela:	¿Y Jorge no puede ir con **ella** el lunes?
Juan:	No, porque ella va al acuario con Isabel y Natalia el lunes.
Ángela:	¿Y Luisa no puede ir con **ellas** el martes?
Juan:	No, porque ellas van con **nosotros** a la feria de libros el martes.
Ángela:	Ah, sí. Tienes razón. Bueno, entonces, ¡hasta el martes!

5 Answers will vary.

6 Answers will vary.

¿RECUERDAS?

NOUN–ADJECTIVE AGREEMENT, p. 22

Práctica

1

1. guapo
2. pequeños
3. inteligente
4. guapa
5. creativas

2 Answers will vary.

Did You Get It? Answer Key

 ¿RECUERDAS?

PLACES AROUND TOWN, p. 23

Práctica

1

1.	park	**2.**	café
3.	movie theater	**4.**	downtown
5.	street	**6.**	concert
7.	theater	**8.**	restaurant

2 Answers will vary.

1.	centro	**2.**	parque
3.	cine	**4.**	café
5.	teatro	**6.**	restaurante
7.	concierto	**8.**	calle

¿RECUERDAS?

STEM–CHANGING VERBS: E ⟶ I, p. 24

Práctica

1. *Mi padre pide una ensalada.*
2. Mis amigos piden el pollo.
3. Tú pides un café.
4. Mis abuelos piden el pescado.
5. Ángela y yo pedimos un pastel.
6. Yo pido las verduras.
7. María pide un café.
8. Ustedes piden el arroz.
9. Raúl pide la carne.
10. Nosotros pedimos las patatas.

Palabras escondidas *Práctica de vocabulario*

Use the words in the following sentence to create words from the **Vocabulario**.
There are at least thirteen possible answers. Can you find more?

Anteayer quemaron discos compactos.

1. _____
2. _____
3. _____
4. _____
5. _____
6. _____
7. _____
8. _____
9. _____
10. _____
11. _____
12. _____
13. _____
14. _____
15. _____
16. _____
17. _____

Correo Electrónico *Vocabulario en contexto*

Fill in the blanks according to the clues to discover a secret word that appears vertically.

1. Para abrir el programa haz **c**____ aquí.
2. **T**____ fotos es divertido.
3. Puedes **q**____ un disco compacto para hacer una copia.
4. La **p**____ demuestra el texto o fotos.
5. Otra palabra que significa «después» es **l**____ .
6. Otro modo (*way*) de hablar con tus amigos es el mensajero **i**____ .
7. Se puede **b**____ una película también en Internet.
8. El **t**____ se usa para escribir texto.
9. Me gusta recibir los **c**____ electrónicos.
10. Si buscas información puedes **n**____ por Internet.
11. El año **p**____ visité a mis amigos en Nueva York.

1.
2.
3.
4.
5.
6.
7.
8.
9.
10.
11.

Unidad 7, Lección 1
Practice Games
32
¡Avancemos! 1
Unit Resource Book

UNIDAD 7 Lección 1
Practice Games

¿Qué hiciste? *Práctica de gramática 1*

Use the clues to fill in the missing letters of the preterite **-er** and **-ir** verb conjugations to discover something that each of these people did recently.

1. Elena y yo c ____ m ____ ____ ____ ____ hamburguesas en la cafetería.

2. Guillermo c ____ rr ____ ____ a clase para no llegar tarde.

3. Yo p ____ d ____ el pastel en el restaurante.

4. Esteban y Eloisa e n ____ o l ____ ____ ____ r ____ ____ todos los regalos para la fiesta.

5. Tú s ____ l ____ ____ ____ ____ con todos los amigos ayer.

6. Ustedes s ____ rv ____ ____ r ____ ____ la comida en la sala pero comimos en el comedor.

7. Eduardo b ____ b ____ ____ mucha agua después del partido.

Código secreto *Gramática en contexto*

David used a secret code to write an e-mail about his dinner date at a fancy restaurant. Use the code key to decipher the note and conjugate the verbs in the preterite.

1% : yo   **3@ : Matilde**   **5& : los camareros**

2# : tú   **4^ : nosotros**

Hola Diego,

Anoche **1%** _____ (salir) _____ a un restaurante con Matilde.
4^ _____ (subir) _____ a la calle Monte Alto para
llegar al restaurante Dorado. **3@** _____ (pedir) _____
el pescado. **1%** _____ (comer) _____ un bistec.
5& _____ (servir) _____ los platos
con mucho estilo (*style*). **3@** _____ (abrir) _____ el
regalo. **1%** _____ (recibir) _____ la cuenta. ¡Cien dólares!
¿**2#** _____ (comer) _____ en el Dorado una vez?

Adiós,
Davíd

¿Quieres ir conmigo? *Práctica de gramática 2*

You've invited Berta, Mario, Ricardo and Tina to go to the amusement park with you. You all decide that whatever you do, you'll all do it together. However, everyone has something to say about what that is. Figure out what the group is going to do by using the clues below. The amusement park layout below will help you.

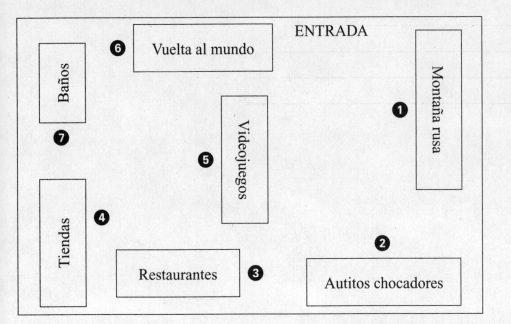

Llegan al parque y tú quieres hacer todo (*do everything*) pero tus amigos...

1 Berta tiene miedo de subirse a la montaña rusa. Mario piensa que es muy divertido. A Ricardo también le encanta. A Tina no le importa (*it doesn't matter to Tina*).

2 A Tina le encantan los autitos chocadores. Berta dice que no los sabe manejar. Mario no quiere subirse. Ricardo se lastimó en los autitos una vez y no quiere subirse.

3 Mario tiene hambre y quiere una hamburguesa. Ricardo y Tina quieren comer también. A Berta no le gusta comer cuando va a los parques de diversiones.

4 Tina no quiere gastar (*spend*) su dinero en las tiendas. Berta quiere comprar unos recuerdos (*souvenirs*). Ricardo quiere una camiseta. A Mario no le importa.

5 Mario quiere jugar a los videojuegos. A Berta no le gustan. A Tina no le importa. Ricardo quiere jugar también.

6 Tina quiere subirse a la vuelta al mundo. Berta tiene miedo subirse. A Ricardo y a Mario no les importa.

CONCLUSIÓN:

Tú les dices a tus amigos que sólo hay un lugar al que todos pueden ir.
Tus amigos están de acuerdo (*agree*).

¿Cuál es el lugar? _____

Computadora escondida (*Hidden computer*) *Todo junto*

Unscramble the words related to the computer.

1. tsiio ____ ____ ____ ____

2. ncooi ____ ____ ____ ____ ____

3. antró ____ ____ ____ ____ ____

4. lacedto ____ ____ ____ ____ ____ ____ ____

5. llpanata ____ ____ ____ ____ ____ ____ ____ ____

6. tenneIrt ____ ____ ____ ____ ____ ____ ____ ____

¡Todos! ¡Nunca!

Find the eight words describing frequency hidden in the word search, then write them on the lines below. Words run horizontal, vertical, and diagonal.

```
S  B  C  S  T  P  S  I  Y  C  Y  X  A  N
A  N  C  R  A  L  L  I  A  T  C  Ó  H  A
H  U  A  L  M  Ú  R  T  E  N  O  C  N  D
A  N  E  S  P  A  Ó  É  L  M  R  M  Y  I
A  C  E  S  O  C  Q  L  E  R  P  A  É  E
L  A  A  L  C  A  L  G  O  I  Z  R  E  B
P  T  M  U  O  Ó  N  L  T  Y  Ó  R  E  I
E  A  L  G  Ú  N  M  P  K  R  N  A  H  L
R  O  D  I  L  L  A  A  N  N  É  D  A  L
U  D  P  N  E  H  L  S  G  A  G  I  S  O
E  S  I  E  B  O  E  F  O  D  L  O  O  A
T  A  M  B  I  É  N  R  C  A  C  Ó  F  É
```

1. _____   2. _____

3. _____   4. _____

5. _____   6. _____

7. _____   8. _____

Te gusta... *Repaso de la lección*

Figure out the seven-letter word that describes something you would probably enjoy. You'll find the seven or eight letters by solving the sentence puzzles. Hint: circle all the letters that the two words from **Vocabulario** have in common, and then eliminate those that are also in the third word.

Seguro que te gusta ____ ____ ____ ____ ____ ____ ____ .

1. This letter is in **anteayer** and **entonces**, but not in **tarde**. ____
2. This letter is in **año** and **ratón**, but not in **icono**. ____
3. This letter is in **navegar** and **levantar**, but not in **conectar**. ____
4. This letter is in **línea** and **mensajero**, but not in **pantalla**. ____
5. This letter is in **luego** and **digital**, but not in **teclado**. ____
6. This letter is in **cámara** and **teclado**, but not in **entonces**. ____
7. This letter is in **Internet** and **electrónico**, but not in **instantáneo**. ____

UNIDAD 7 Lección 1

Practice Games

Partes de palabras *Práctica de vocabulario*

Identify the following–two word combinations from **Vocabulario** using the parts of the combinations shown in each box.

1. ___ ___ [N G] ___ ___   ___ ___ [E D] ___ .

2. ___ ___ [É F] ___ ___ ___ ___   ___ ___ ___ [U L] ___ ___

3. ___ ___ [N T] ___ ___ ___   ___ [U S] ___

4. ¡ ___ [U É] ___ ___ ___ ___ [T I] ___ ___ !

¡Lotería! *Vocabulario en contexto*

Play this game alone or with a friend. Use coins to mark your answers to the clues below. The first player with markers across three squares (horizontally, diagonally or vertically) wins.

Clues:

1. Quiero ir al **a**_____ a ver diferentes tipos de peces. _____

2. Un famoso **p**___ **d**___ **d**___ es Six Flags. _____

3. Me gusta ver a los monos (*monkeys*) jugando cuando voy al **z**___ . _____

4. Esa película solamente se puede ver en el **c**___ . _____

5. En el **m**___ se pueden ver cosas antiguas (*old*). _____

6. No quiero subir a la **m**___ **r**___ porque tengo miedo. _____

7. Tomo muchas fotos con mi **c**___ . _____

8. La **v**___ **a**___ **m**___ va muy despacio. _____

9. Ya compré mi **b**___ para entrar al parque. _____

10. Me gusta manejar los **a**___ **c**___ porque son muy divertidos. _____

11. La **f**___ estatal de Texas es muy grande. _____

12. ¿Puedo llamarte a tu **t**___ **c**___ cuando ya me quiero ir a la casa? _____

Lugares a ir, cosas a hacer *Práctica de gramática 1*

Circle the correct preterite form of each verb. Then, write the bolded letters from the answers you chose to find out Emilio's favorite time of day. Some letters are already provided.

1. Felipa y yo _____ al museo ayer.

    imos   fu**imos**   **vayamos**

2. Gerardo _____ a la casa de su amigo.

    fue   **i**y**a**   v**a**ya

3. ¿Qué _____ el fin de semana pasada?

    hacest**e**   **hi**jaste   hicis**te**

4. Mona _____ su tarea antes de la cena.

    hago   **hizo**   he**cho**

A L ___ ___ ___ R ___ O

Crucigrama *Gramática en contexto*

Use the correct preterite forms of **ser**, **ir**, or **hacer** to complete the sentences and fill in the crossword puzzle.

Horizontal (*across*)

1. Gabi y Fernando _____ sus camas por la mañana.

3. Amistad _____ esquí acuático con mis padres.

5. Tú _____ a la piscina con Paco ayer. ¿No?

Abajo (*down*)

1. Nosotros _____ la tarea después de la película.

2. Yo _____ el ganador del partido.

4. Yo _____ clic en el ratón pero no salió nada en la computadora.

6. Los exámenes _____ muy difíciles.

7. Salvador y yo _____ a la biblioteca para jugar con las computadoras.

UNIDAD 7 Lección 2 — Practice Games

¡Avancemos! 1
Unit Resource Book

Familias de palabras *Práctica de gramática 2*

Use twelve of the words from the box to complete the sentences.

luego	para ti	a la escuela	anteayer
contigo	un momento	cerca de la televisión	
debajo del sofá	el año pasado		para Javier
la semana pasada	anoche	contigo	
lejos del partido	todavía está		pero no puedo
a Inés	conmigo	con Alberto	
me llamo	tal vez	en coche	al cine

1. Voy a la tienda. ¿Quieres ir _____?
2. No sé donde está mi dinero. Tal vez está _____ .
3. No voy al parque sola. Voy _____ .
4. No quiero mirar el béisbol. Estoy _____ .
5. No quiero comer mi hamburguesa. Voy a dársela _____ .
6. Quiero ver la película nueva. Quiero ir _____ .
7. El libro no es para mí. Es _____ , porque él quiere leero.
8. Me gusta conducir! Siempre voy _____ .
9. Es tu cumpleaños, y tengo regalo _____ .
10. Puedo ver el programa. Estoy _____ .
11. ¿Vas a Argentina? Quiero ir _____ .
12. Cinco días de la semana, necesitamos ir _____ .

UNIDAD 7 Lección 2   Practice Games

Guía turística *Todo junto*

You are leading your family on a tour of a Spanish-speaking country. You must figure out which sites are the best to visit by reading the travel brochures. Draw a line to match each brochure with the place it describes.

Puedes jugar juegos, ganar precios, comer dulces y comprar mucho.	¡Ves peces de todas las formas! ¡Imagina que estás en el mar!	Ves pinturas y cosas viejas. Aprendes del pasado.	¡Leones, tigres y osos! ¡Ay de mí!

El museo	La feria	El zoológico	El acuario

El parque de diversiones *Lectura cultural*

Mariposa has lost her friends in the amusement park. She is trying to remember
where everyone has gone. Help her sentences make sense by writing the correct from
of the underlined verbs in the blanks.

1. Cesia y José fue _____ a la montaña rusa.

2. Luciana fueron _____ a la vuelta al mundo.

3. Yo hicimos _____ las juegos.

4. Todos nosotros fuiste _____ a los autitos chocadores.

5. Humberto y yo hizo _____ muchas cosas.

6. Manuel, ¿Adónde fuimos _____ tú?

Rimas *Repaso de la leccion*

Read the following poem. Underline the prepositions.

Fui al parque de diversiones.
El parque está al lado de
la tienda de televisores.

Fui a los autitos chocadores.
Los hombres de vender boletos
no son muy trabajadores.

Mañana quiero ir al acuario.
¿Por qué no vienes tú conmigo?

Practice Games Answer Key

PAGE 31
Práctica de vocabulario

possible words: semana, pasada, pasado, entonces, tarde, tomar, Internet, mandar, correos, conectar, quemar, icono, ratón, cámara

PAGE 32
Vocabulario en contexto

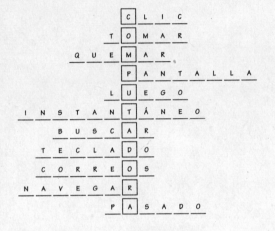

PAGE 33
Práctica de gramática 1

1. comimos
2. corrió
3. pedí
4. envolvieron
5. saliste
6. sirvieron
7. bebió

PAGE 34
Gramática en contexto

Yo, salí, Nosotros, subimos, Matilde, pidió, Yo, comí, Los camareros, sirvieron, Matilde, abrió, Yo, recibí, Tú, comiste

PAGE 35
Práctica de gramática 2

Los baños

PAGE 36
Todo junto

1. sitio
2. icono
3. ratón
4. teclado
5. pantalla
6. Internet

Practice Games Answer Key

UNIDAD 7 Lección 1

PAGE 37
Lectura

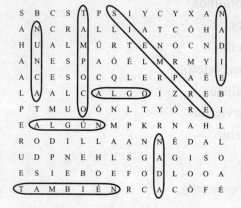

1. nunca
2. tampoco
3. siempre
4. nadie
5. algo
6. algún
7. nada
8. también

PAGE 38
Repaso de la lección

N-A-V-E-G-A-R

Practice Games Answer Key

PAGE 39

Práctica de vocabulario

1. Tengo miedo.
2. teléfono celular
3. montaña rusa
4. ¡Qué lástima!

PAGE 40

Vocabulario en contexto

Clues:

1. acuario
2. parque de diversión
3. zoológico
4. cine
5. museo
6. montaña rusa
7. cámara
8. vuelta al mundo
9. boleto
10. autitos chocadores
11. feria
12. teléfono celular

PAGE 41

Práctica de gramática 1

1. Fuimos
2. fue
3. hiciste
4. hizo

ALMUERZO

PAGE 42

Gramática en contexto

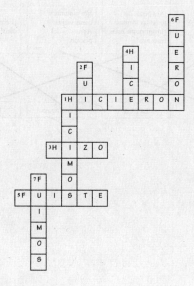

PAGE 43

Práctica de gramática 2

1. conmigo
2. debajo del sofá
3. con Alberto
4. lejos del partido
5. a Inés
6. al cine
7. para Javier
8. en coche
9. para ti
10. cerca de la televisión
11. contigo
12. a la escuela

Practice Games Answer Key

PAGE 44

Todo junto

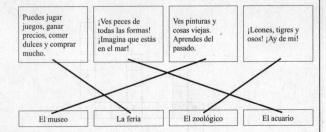

PAGE 45

Lectura cultural

1. fueron
2. fue
3. hice
4. fuimos
5. hicimos
6. fuiste

PAGE 46

Repaso de la lección

Poem: underline al, de, al, de, de (1st stanza), a, de (2nd stanza), al, conmigo (3rd stanza)

Video Activities *Vocabulario*

PRE-VIEWING ACTIVITY

Before you watch the video, answer these questions about using the Internet.

1 How do you use the Internet to communicate with people?

_____

_____

2 What are some other ways you use the Internet?

_____

_____

3 What are some tools involved in using a computer?

_____

_____

4 What problems might you have when you use a computer?

_____

_____

VIEWING ACTIVITY

Read the statements below before you watch the video. While you watch, write (**T**) if the statement is true, and (**F**) if it is false.

1. Mariano compra comida en el cybercafe.	T	F
2. Florencia escribe su dirección electrónica.	T	F
3. El ratón funciona bién.	T	F
4. Luciana está conectada al Internet.	T	F
5. La bebida de Florencia se cae en el ratón.	T	F
6. Florencia no puede mandar las fotos de su cámara digital.	T	F

Video Activities *Vocabulario*

POST-VIEWING ACTIVITY

After you watch the video, use the words in the word bank to complete each sentence.

cámara digital	cybercafé	dirreción electrónica	disco	en línea	ratón

1. No hay bebidas porque no es restaurante, es un _____ .

2. Cuando Florencia se conecta al Internet, ella escribe su _____ .

3. Después de conectarse, Florencia está _____ .

4. Florencia necesita ayuda porque el _____ no funciona.

5. Florencia manda las fotos que tomó con su _____ .

6. Florencia necesita el _____ que tiene las fotos.

52

Unidad 7, Lección 1
Video Activities

¡**Avancemos! 1**
Unit Resource Book

UNIDAD 7 Lección 1

Video Activities

Video Activities *Telehistoria escena 1*

PRE-VIEWING ACTIVITY

Imagine you have a friend who has an e–mail account, but doesn't know how to send an e-mail. Write a short paragraph explaining to your friend, step by step, how to create and send an e-mail.

OR

If you do not know how to send an e-mail, write two questions you would ask a friend who knows how.

_____

_____

_____

_____

_____

_____

_____

_____

VIEWING ACTIVITY

Scan the list of countries below before watching the video. While watching the video, put in chronological order the places to which Alicia's T-shirt has traveled.

_____ Puerto Rico

_____ Argentina

_____ España

_____ la República Dominicana

_____ México

_____ Ecuador

_____ Texas

Video Activities *Telehistoria escena 1*

POST-VIEWING ACTIVITY

Choose the word or phrase that best completes each of the following sentences.

1. Alicia mandó _____ a Florencia.

   a. un autógrafo de Trini Salgado

   b. un mensajero instantáneo

   c. un correo electrónico

2. Alicia es _____ de Florencia.

   a. una prima

   b. una amiga

   c. una hermana

3. Alicia vive en _____.

   a. Texas

   b. Florida

   c. Puerto Rico

4. Mariano y Florencia viven en _____.

   a. Miami

   b. Puebla

   c. Buenos Aires

5. Sandra fue la _____ en recibir la camiseta de Alicia.

   a. primera

   b. segunda

   c. tercera

6. Muchos amigos de Alicia _____ a Trini Salgado.

   a. buscaron

   b. mandaron

   c. llamaron

7. Trini Salgado está ahora en _____.

   a. Miami

   b. Puebla

   c. Buenos Aires

8. Alicia es _____ de fútbol.

   a. cancha

   b. maestra

   c. jugadora

UNIDAD 7 Lección 1

Video Activities

Unidad 7, Lección 1
Video Activities

54

¡Avancemos! 1
Unit Resource Book

Video Activities *Telehistoria escena 2*

PRE-VIEWING ACTIVITY

Answer the following questions about the Internet.

❶ How often do you use the Internet?

_____

_____

❷ What features do you use on the Internet?

_____

_____

❸ Where do you access the Internet?

_____

_____

❹ How would your life be different without the Internet?

_____

_____

VIEWING ACTIVITY

Scan the activities listed below before watching the video. While you watch, indicate with a checkmark (🕐) whether the characters did each activity **ayer** (*yesterday*) or the activity is happening **hoy** (*today*).

AYER	HOY	
_____	_____	**1.** ir al cibercafé otra vez
_____	_____	**2.** volver a casa
_____	_____	**3.** navegar por Internet en casa
_____	_____	**4.** no recibir mucha información de Trini
_____	_____	**5.** recibir un correo electrónico
_____	_____	**6.** compartir muchas ideas
_____	_____	**7.** tener que navegar por Internet

Video Activities *Telehistoria escena 2*

POST-VIEWING ACTIVITY

Complete each sentence with the appropriate phrase.

1. Anoche Florencia recibió _____ .

    a. muchas ideas.

2. Florencia volvió _____ .

    b. la cámara digital.

3. Florencia y Alicia compartieron _____ .

    c. para buscar más información de Trini.

4. Mariano y Florencia van a _____ .

    d. cuando Trini va a estar en el estadio.

5. Florencia no sabe _____ .

    e. tomar más fotos.

6. Mariano y Florencia van al cibercafé _____ .

    f. otro correo electrónico de Alicia.

7. Mariano y Florencia perdieron _____ .

    g. buscar a Trini en el estadio.

8. Ahora Mariano y Florencia no pueden _____ .

    h. a casa después de estar en el cibercafé.

Video Activities *Telehistoria escena 3*

PRE-VIEWING ACTIVITY

Answer the following questions based on what you already know about Florencia and Mariano.

1 In scene two, Mariano and Florencia leave the restaurant to go to an Internet café. What did they leave behind?

_____

2 Based on how the second scene ends, how do you think the next scene will unfold? Write a short paragraph about what you think might happen.

_____

_____

_____

_____

VIEWING ACTIVITY

Read the following statements before watching the video. While you watch, indicate whether each statement is true (T) or false (F).

1. El camarero tiene la cámara digital de Mariano y Florencia.   T   F

2. Mariano y Florencia siempre necesitan algo.   T   F

3. Quieren ver a Trini a las cuatro de la tarde.   T   F

4. El camarero dice que Trini viene al Parque de la Costa en El Tigre.   T   F

5. Nadie encontró a Trini en los Estados Unidos.   T   F

6. Alguien recibió el autógrafo de Trini en Puerto Rico.   T   F

UNIDAD 7 Lección 1   Video Activities

Video Activities *Telehistoria escena 3*

POST-VIEWING ACTIVITY

Choose the word from the box that best completes each of the following sentences.

el café	la cámara digital	el autógrafo	la fecha	el sábado	nada	la hora

1. Mariano y Florencia perdieron _____ .

2. Ellos encontraron lo que perdieron en _____ .

3. El camarero no sabe _____ del estadio.

4. Trini va a estar en el Parque de la Costa en El Tigre _____ .

5. Mariano piensa que Florencia va a obtener _____ de Trini.

Unidad 7, Lección 1
Video Activities

58

UNIDAD 7 Lección 1

Video Activities

¡**Avancemos!** 1
Unit Resource Book

Video Activities *Vocabulario*

PRE-VIEWING ACTIVITY

1 Where are some places of interest you like to go for fun?

_____

_____

2 What are some places of interest that you do not enjoy visiting?

_____

_____

3 What are your favorite things to do in an amusement park?

_____

_____

4 What activities or rides do you avoid in amusement parks?

_____

_____

VIEWING ACTIVITY

Read the items below before watching the video. Then, while you watch, put them in the order in which Florencia and Mariano discuss them.

_____ **1.** los autitos chocadores

_____ **2.** la montaña rusa

_____ **3.** el museo

_____ **4.** el parque de diversiones

_____ **5.** la vuelta al mundo

_____ **6.** el zoológico

Video Activities *Vocabulario*

POST-VIEWING ACTIVITY

After you watch the video, match each item to the correct description.

1. Algunas personas piensan que mueve demasiado rapidamente _____ .

2. Tiene mucho arte _____ .

3. Hay muchos carros conduciendo en el mismo lugar _____ .

4. Es un gran círculo _____ .

5. Tiene muchos animales _____ .

6. Es donde Luciana quiere ir con Mariano _____ .

a. el museo

b. la montaña rusa

c. el parque de diversiones

d. los autitos chocadores

e. la vuelta al mundo

f. el zoológico

Video Activities *Telehistoria escena 1*

PRE-VIEWING ACTIVITY

Answer the following questions.

1 How do you communicate with your friends when you aren't around them?

_____

_____

2 How often do you use each of these forms of communication?

_____

_____

3 Which of these forms of communication do you use to make and modify plans with friends?

_____

_____

4 How would you make plans with friends if you didn't have access to one of these forms of communication?

_____

_____

VIEWING ACTIVITY

Read the following phrases before watching the video. While you watch, indicate whether
Florencia or Mariano says each phrase by placing a checkmark (🕐) under the appropriate
name. Hint: The phrases may be worded differently in the video.

Florencia	Mariano	
_____	_____	Veo la vuelta al mundo.
_____	_____	Tengo que llamarlo.
_____	_____	No te veo.
_____	_____	Estamos cerca de la vuelta al mundo.
_____	_____	Yo lo compré también.
_____	_____	Veo la montaña rusa.
_____	_____	¿Dónde está él?
_____	_____	Ya compramos nuestros boletos.

Video Activities *Telehistoria escena 1*

POST-VIEWING ACTIVITY

Complete each sentence with the appropriate phrase.

1. Florencia no sabe _____.

2. Florencia habla por _____.

3. Todos ya compraron _____.

4. Todos ya están _____.

5. Mariano y Luciana no están _____.

6. Florencia está _____.

7. Mariano y Luciana están _____.

8. Florencia encuentra _____.

a. lejos de Florencia.

b. a ellos delante de los autitos chocadores.

c. más cerca de la vuelta al mundo.

d. dónde está Mariano.

e. sus boletos.

f. teléfono celular con Mariano.

g. en el Parque de la Costa.

h. cerca de la moñtana rusa

UNIDAD 7 Lección 2

Video Activities

Unidad 7, Lección 2
Video Activities

62

¡Avancemos! 1
Unit Resource Book

Video Activities *Telehistoria escena 2*

PRE-VIEWING ACTIVITY

Answer the following questions.

1 What famous person do you most admire?

_____

2 Why do you admire this person?

_____

_____

3 Where would you most likely run into this person?

_____

_____

4 What would you say to this person if you met him or her?

_____

_____

VIEWING ACTIVITY

Read the list of places below before watching the video. While you watch the video, check off (🕐) each place that Mariano, Florencia, and Luciana visit.

_____ la feria

_____ la vuelta al mundo

_____ la montaña rusa

_____ los autitos chocadores

_____ el restaurante

_____ la ventanilla de información

Video Activities *Telehistoria escena 2*

POST-VIEWING ACTIVITY

Choose the word or phrase that best completes each of the following sentences.

1. Mariano va a la ventanilla a ver dónde pueden _____.

    a. encontrar un restaurante

    b. tomar fotos

    c. encontrar a Trini

2. El señor de la ventanilla dice que Trini fue _____.

    a. a un restaurante

    b. a la vuelta al mundo

    c. al acuario

3. Mariano, Florencia y Luciana van allí pero Trini _____.

    a. no está

    b. no quiere hablar con ellos

    c. está ocupada

4. Mariano toma un foto de Luciana delante de _____.

    a. la vuelta al mundo

    b. los autitos chocadores

    c. la feria

5. El señor dice a Florencia que Trini fue _____.

    a. a bailar

    b. a comer

    c. a subir a la montaña rusa

6. Ellos van _____ pero Trini también no está allí.

    a. a la feria

    b. a la montaña rusa

    c. al restaurante

7. _____ piensa que no van a encontrar a Trini.

    a. Mariano

    b. Florencia

    c. Luciana

Video Activities *Telehistoria escena 3*

PRE-VIEWING ACTIVITY

Answer the following questions about how you and your friends pay for things.

1 Do your friends ever pay your way to an event or for food?

_____

_____

2 Do you ever pay a friend's way to an event or for food?

_____

_____

3 Explain why you do or do not share expenses with your friends.

_____

_____

4 Do you think the way that you pay for things with friends is culturally or personally influenced?

_____

_____

VIEWING ACTIVITY

Read the sentences below before watching the video. Then, while you watch the video, check off (🕐) each phrase that you hear.

_____ **1.** Voy a comprar unas ensaladas.

_____ **2.** Comprás un refresco para mí.

_____ **3.** Compré unas empanadas para tí.

_____ **4.** ¿Te gustaría venir conmigo a buscar al señor?

_____ **5.** Puedes encontrarnos allí.

_____ **6.** Señorita Trini Salgado, la esperan en la puerta.

_____ **7.** ¡Qué horrible!

Video Activities *Telehistoria escena 3*

POST-VIEWING ACTIVITY

Indicate whether the following statements are true (T) or false (F).

1. Luciana piensa que las empanadas son ricas. T F

2. Florencia no tiene hambre. T F

3. Luciana fue a comprar comida para todos. T F

4. Luciana pide un refresco para Mariano. T F

5. A Mariano le gustaría ir con Luciana a buscar a Trini. T F

6. Mariano y Florencia encontraron a Trini delante de los autitos chocadores. T F

7. Ellos conocen a Trini Salgado, la jugadora de fútbol. T F

8. Mariano, Florencia y Luciana están contentos. T F

UNIDAD 7 Lección 2

Video Activities

Unidad 7, Lección 2
Video Activities

66

¡Avancemos! 1
Unit Resource Book

Video Activities Answer Key

VOCABULARIO pp. 51–52

PRE-VIEWING ACTIVITY

Answers will vary. Sample answers:

1. I communicate with people over the Internet by sending e-mails.
2. The Internet can also be used to do research.
3. The mouse and keyboard are tools involved when using a computer.
4. There are many problems associated with computer use, such as problems connecting to the Internet.

VIEWING ACTIVITY

1. F
2. T
3. F
4. T
5. F
6. T

POST-VIEWING ACTIVITY

1. cybercafé
2. dirreción electrónica
3. en línea
4. ratón
5. cámara digital
6. disco

TELEHISTORIA ESCENA 1, pp. 53–54

PRE-VIEWING ACTIVITY

Answers will vary. Possible answer: Go to your e-mail site. Log in to your account with your username and password. Once you are logged in, click on the "new e-mail" icon. Then type the e-mail address of the person to whom you are writing. Type your message in the space below. Finally, click the "send" icon, and your e-mail will be sent!

Possible answer to alternative question: How do you start sending an e-mail? How do you make sure an e-mail gets to the right person?

VIEWING ACTIVITY

Puerto Rico 3

Argentina 7

España 4

la República Dominicana 6

México 2

Ecuador 5

Texas 1

POST-VIEWING ACTIVITY

1. c
2. b
3. b
4. c
5. a
6. a
7. c
8. c

TELEHISTORIA ESCENA 2, pp. 55–56

PRE-VIEWING ACTIVITY

1. Answers will vary. Possible answer: I use the Internet every day.
2. Answers will vary. Possible answer: I send e-mails to my friends and read the school newspaper online. I also use the Internet to do research for my homework.
3. Answers will vary. Possible answer: I log on to the Internet at school, in the library, and at home.
4. Answers will vary. Possible answer: I would use my cell phone more to communicate with my friends. I would also use the library to do research for my assignments.

VIEWING ACTIVITY

1. hoy
2. ayer
3. hoy
4. ayer
5. ayer
6. ayer
7. hoy

POST-VIEWING ACTIVITY

1. f
2. h
3. a
4. g
5. d
6. c
7. b
8. e

TELEHISTORIA ESCENA 3, pp. 57–58

PRE-VIEWING ACTIVITY

1. They left their digital camera.
2. Answers will vary. Possible answer: Florencia will realize that she doesn't have her camera anymore when she decides she wants to take a picture of her friend. Florencia and Mariano will rush back to the restaurant. They will find the camera on the table where they left it and will notice the poster advertising Trini Salgado's conference. They will go to see Trini and get the soccer player's autograph for Alicia.

VIEWING ACTIVITY

1. T
2. F
3. F
4. T
5. T
6. F

POST-VIEWING ACTIVITY

1. la cámara digital
2. el café
3. nada
4. el sábado
5. el autógrafo

VOCABULARIO pp. 59–60

PRE-VIEWING ACTIVITY

Answers will vary. Sample answers:

1. I like to go to the aquarium.
2. I do not enjoy visiting amusement parks.
3. I like to eat cotton candy at amusement parks.
4. I do not go on the Ferris wheel.

VIEWING ACTIVITY

1. 6
2. 4
3. 2
4. 3
5. 5
6. 1

POST-VIEWING ACTIVITY

1. b
2. a
3. d
4. e
5. f
6. c

TELEHISTORIA ESCENA 1, pp 61–62

PRE-VIEWING ACTIVITY

1. Answers will vary. Possible answer: I use a computer to send e-mails and instant messages to my friends and a cell phone to talk to them.
2. Answers will vary. Possible answer: I send e-mails and instant messages to my friends every day. I use my cell phone every day—mostly in the evening.
3. Answers will vary. Possible answer: I usually use my cell phone when making plans with friends.
4. Answers will vary. Possible answer: I would have to make better plans with friends over the phone before leaving the house. We would have to have a definite place to meet each other.

Video Activities Answer Key

VIEWING ACTIVITY

Veo la vuelta al mundo: Florencia

Tengo que llamarlo: Florencia

No te veo: Mariano

Estamos cerca de la vuelta al mundo: Mariano

Yo lo compré también: Florencia

Veo la montaña rusa: Mariano

¿Dónde está él?: Florencia

Ya compramos nuestros boletos: Mariano

POST-VIEWING ACTIVITY

1. d	**2.** f
3. e	**4.** g
5. a	**6.** h
7. c	**8.** b

TELEHISTORIA ESCENA 2, pp. 63–64

PRE-VIEWING ACTIVITY

1. Answers will vary. Possible answer: I really admire _____.

2. Answers will vary. Possible answer: I admire her because she is a really good athlete with lots of talent and drive.

3. Answers will vary. Possible answer: I would probably run into her at an auditorium in a big city.

4. Answers will vary. Possible answer: You are so talented! May I have your autograph?

VIEWING ACTIVITY

la feria

la vuelta al mundo 🕐

la montaña rusa

los autitos chocadores

el restaurante 🕐

la ventanilla de información 🕐

POST-VIEWING ACTIVITY

1. c	**2.** b
3. a	**4.** a
5. b	**6.** c
7. c	

TELEHISTORIA ESCENA 3, pp. 65–66

PRE-VIEWING ACTIVITY

1. Answers will vary. Possible answer: Yes, my friends sometimes pay for me.

2. Answers will vary. Possible answer: Yes, sometimes I pay for my friends.

3. Answers will vary. Possible answer: My friends and I like to share expenses because sometimes one of us doesn't have money. If we share expenses, we get to do more things together.

4. Answers will vary. Possible answer: I think that the way I pay for things with friends is personally influenced.

VIEWING ACTIVITY

1. Voy a comprar unas ensaladas.

2. Compras un refresco para mí. 🕐

3. Compré unas empanadas para tí.

4. ¿Te gustaría venir conmigo a buscar al señor?

5. Puedes encontrarnos allí. 🕐

6. Señorita Trini Salgado, la esperan en la puerta. 🕐

7. ¡Qué horrible!

POST-VIEWING ACTIVITY

1. T	**2.** F
3. T	**4.** T
5. F	**6.** F
7. F	**8.** F

Video Scripts

VOCABULARIO

Mariano: Hola, yo soy Mariano y mi amiga se llama Florencia. Estamos en un cibercafé.

Clerk: Hola, chicos. ¿Puedo ayudar?

Florencia: ¿Podemos usar una computadora?

Mariano: ¿Y, tiene usted algunas galletas?

Clerk: No, no tenemos ninguna comida.

Mariano: ¿Tiene usted algo para beber?

Clerk: No, no tenemos nada para beber.

Florencia: Hay computadoras, ¿no?

Clerk: Sí, hay algunas allí.

Mariano: ¿Usaste las computadoras aquí antes?

Florencia: Sí, usé una computadora ayer. Primero, miro la pantalla... conecto al Internet... escribo mi dirección electrónica... estoy en línea... navego por Internet un rato... entonces veo la página Web que quiero, hago clic al icono... pero el ratón... hago clic otra vez... ¡y nada! Entonces, llamo a alguien para ayudarme... pero nadie viene... Veo mi mensajero instantáneo... ¡y allí está Luciana! Quiero escribir algo, pero tampoco puedo. Por fin, viene el chico a ayudarme... Entonces, ¿el ratón?... Sí, todo está bien. ¡Y yo estoy feliz!

Mariano: Uy, ¿en el teclado?

Florencia: Hoy tomé unas fotos con mi cámara digital, y las quemé en un disco. ¿Dónde está el disco? Ah! aquí está... y, mando las fotos.

Mariano: Ah, antes de ir a la casa. ¿Un refresco, por favor?

TELEHISTORIA ESCENA 1

Florencia: ¡Mariano! Mirá, tengo un correo electrónico de Alicia.

Mariano: ¿Quién es Alicia? Es la chica de Miami, ¿no?

Florencia: Sí, mi amiga, la jugadora de fútbol.

Mariano: ¿Qué dice? Florencia, no puedo ver la pantalla.

Florencia: Alicia quiere el autógrafo de Trini Salgado en su camiseta.

Mariano: ¡La entiendo! ¡Qué bárbaro tener el autógrafo de una jugadora de fútbol famosa como Trini Salgado! ¿Puedo tener la dirección electrónica de Alicia?

Florencia: Ella y sus amigos buscaron a Trini para pedir su autógrafo, pero no es fácil. Alicia mandó la camiseta a Sandra, una amiga que vive en Texas.

Mariano: ¿En Texas?

Florencia: Sí, y después Sandra la mandó a un amigo de Puebla, en México, pero tampoco la encontró.

Mariano: ¿Y entonces?

Florencia: Luego su amigo de México mandó la camiseta a Puerto Rico. Más tarde, sus amigos mandaron la camiseta a España, y entonces a Ecuador y a la República Dominicana.

Mariano: ¡La camiseta de Alicia viaja mucho!

Florencia: Pero... después de todo, no tienen el autógrafo. Y por fin, anteayer la mandaron aquí a Buenos Aires. Porque... ¡Trini está aquí!

Video Scripts

TELEHISTORIA ESCENA 2

Mariano: Florencia, ¿ahora, qué va a pasar con la camiseta de Alicia?

Florencia: Anoche cuando volví a casa recibí otro correo electrónico de Alicia. Aquí está. Compartimos muchas ideas anoche... Escribió que debemos buscar a Trini en el estadio.

Mariano: Pero... ¿Cuándo?

Florencia: No sé, no recibí mucha información. Tenemos que navegar por Internet para buscar la fecha y la hora. ¿Salimos para el cibercafé?

TELEHISTORIA ESCENA 3

Florencia: ¡Señor, por favor! ¿Tiene usted mi cámara?

Waiter: Sí, sí... tranquila. Aquí está. ¿Qué pasa? ¿Necesitan algo?

Mariano: No, nada. Gracias. Queremos ir al estadio para ver a Trini Salgado, pero no sabemos ni la fecha ni la hora. Nadie sabe cuándo va a llegar ella.

Florencia: Usted tampoco sabe, ¿no?

Waiter: No sé nada del estadio, pero sé que Trini Salgado va a estar en el Parque de la Costa, en el Tigre, el sábado.

Florencia: ¿Sí? ¿Cómo lo sabe?

Waiter: Mirá, allí dice.

Mariano: ¡Florencia! Nadie encontró a Trini... ni en los Estados Unidos ... ni en Puerto Rico... tampoco en España. Pero ahora, vos vas a tener el autógrafo. ¡Qué bárbaro!

Video Scripts

VOCABULARIO

Florencia: ¡Hola! Ah, Hola Mariano...

Mariano: Hola, Florencia. ¿Cómo estás? Me gustaría salir con Luciana el fin de semana. Pero, no sé adónde.

Florencia: ¿Por qué no van al zoológico?

Mariano: Mnnn, no me gusta el zoológico.

Florencia: Entonces, ¿al museo? ...¡o a la feria del libro!

Mariano: No sé... y, ¿cómo la invito?

Florencia: Muy fácil. "Decís": Luciana, ¿querés acompañarme a la feria del libro? Mariano, un momento, tengo otra llamada. ¿Hola? Ah Luciana, hola...

Luciana: Hola, Florencia, acabo de encontrar tu número de teléfono celular. Ya no tengo que dejar mensajes con tu mamá. ¿Mariano está allí?

Florencia: No, no.

Luciana: Quiero invitar a Mariano al parque de diversiones el sábado, pero no contesta su teléfono.

Florencia: Luciana, un momento. ¿Mariano? ¡Luciana y vos deben ir al parque de diversiones!

Mariano: ¿Al parque de diversiones? ¡No! Tengo miedo de subir a la montaña rusa.

Florencia: ¿Y no te gusta la vuelta al mundo?

Mariano: Tampoco. ¡Qué miedo!

Florencia: ¿y los autitos chocadores?

Mariano: ¡Ah, Florencia! Sí, me gustaría salir con Luciana... pero, ¿por qué al parque de diversiones?

Luciana: ¿Hola, Mariano? No soy Florencia, soy Luciana. ¿Te gustaría ir al parque de diversiones?

Mariano: ¡Hola, Luciana! Bueno, sí, me gustaría mucho. ¿Florencia? ¿Querés ir? Entonces, el sábado.

TELEHISTORIA ESCENA 1

Florencia: ¿Dónde está Mariano? Tengo que llamarlo a su teléfono celular.

Mariano: Hola, Florencia. Sí, Luciana y yo estamos en el parque de La Costa. Compramos nuestros boletos.

Florencia: Yo también. ¿Pueden ver la montaña rusa?

Mariano: Sí, pero estamos más cerca de la vuelta al mundo.

Florencia: Ahora veo la vuelta al mundo. Ustedes deben estar cerca.

Mariano: No te veo.

Luciana: ¿Por qué no encontramos a Florencia delante de los autitos chocadores?

TELEHISTORIA ESCENA 2

Luciana: ¡Ay! Che Mariano, ¿dónde fuiste?

Mariano: Yo fui a ver dónde podemos encontrar a Trini. Sé dónde está.

Luciana: ¿Cómo lo sabes?

Mariano: Fue el señor de la ventanilla. Él dice que Trini fue a la vuelta al mundo.

Florencia: Mariano, ¡qué bárbaro! ¡Vamos! El señor dice que Trini y sus amigos fueron a comer.

Video Scripts

Mariano: ¿Trini fue a comer? ¡Ay no! ¿Qué podemos hacer? Tenemos que ir a buscarla otra vez.

Luciana: Fuimos a la vuelta al mundo, fuimos al restaurante. ¿Dónde está Trini? Nunca la vamos a encontrar.

TELEHISTORIA ESCENA 3

Luciana: ¡Mmmm... empanadas!, ¡Qué ricas! Voy a comprar unas. ¿Florencia y Mariano, quieren algo?

Florencia: Gracias Luciana, ¿por qué no comprás un refresco para mí y unas empanadas para nosotros dos? Y Mariano, ¿te gustaría venir conmigo a buscar a Trini a los autitos chocadores? Luciana, podés encontrarnos allí.

Voice over speakers: Atención por favor, señorita Trini Salgado, por favor, la buscan en la puerta, señorita Trini Salgado.

Florencia y Mariano: ¡Vamos!

Mujer: Señor... ¡yo soy Trini Salgado!

Florencia: ¿Trini Salgado? ¿La jugadora de fútbol?

Mujer: ¿La jugadora de fútbol?

Luciana: ¿Quieren empanadas?

COMPARACIÓN CULTURAL VIDEO

After a week of hard work, everybody deserves a fun weekend. Here you are going to see how people spend their weekends in Buenos Aires, in Mexico, and also in Puerto Rico.

Argentina

Whether sitting in a park watching the dance of tango, or playing soccer, Buenos Aires can provide entertainment for everyone.

During the weekends Argentineans go to theaters, cinemas, and museums. They visit the zoo, or go to the River Plate Stadium to see a soccer match. Or, listening to a man with a guitar in the street can be as much fun as any other cultural activity.

They go see monuments to their national history, like el **Obelisco**, or visit historical buildings like the government house, **La Casa Rosada**.

Mexico

Mexico's colonial and indigenous heritage is evident almost everywhere in Mexico City. The city has 68 plazas, 53 museums, and 1500 historical buildings. With such a picture, deciding what to do and where to go during the weekends is an adventure in itself.

Those who like history visit the **Museo de Antropología**, or they go to the **Zócalo**, the main plaza and center of the city. Mexicans also go to this plaza to celebrate their independence every September, or to see concerts.

Puerto Rico

For Puerto Ricans, **El Morro** is more than a major tourist attraction. This fort built by the Spanish in the 1500's, in what is now Old San Juan, is a popular place for flying kites, cycling, and going for a picnic.

You have seen how Argentineans in Buenos Aires appreciate their city's attractions, how Mexicans enjoy their colonial and indigenous heritage in Mexico City, and how Puerto Ricans in Old San Juan relax and picnic in front of a former military fort. Just like visitors do, local people also enjoy their hometowns and the historical sites in their cities.

Audio Scripts

UNIDAD 7, LECCIÓN 1
TEXTBOOK SCRIPTS
TXT CD 7
LEVEL 1B TXT CD 2

PRESENTACIÓN DE VOCABULARIO

Level 1 Textbook pp. 356-357

Level 1B Textbook pp. 166-168

TXT CD 7, Track 1

A. ¡Hola! Me llamo Florencia. Anteayer pasé un rato con mis amigos Mariano y Luciana. Tomamos fotos delante de la Casa Rosada.

B. Hoy, Mariano y yo estamos en la biblioteca. Aquí navegamos por Internet, usamos el mensajero instantáneo y mandamos correos electrónicos. Quiero mandar las fotos que tomé anteayer.

C. Es fácil mandarlas y no cuesta nada. Primero conecto a Internet. Cuando estoy en línea, escribo un correo electrónico con las fotos. Por fin, pongo la dirección electrónica de mi amiga y hago clic en el icono para mandarlas.

¡A RESPONDER!

Level 1 Textbook p. 357

TXT CD 7, Track 2

Level 1B Textbook p. 168

Level 1B TXT CD 2, Track 1

Florencia compró una computadora nueva. Escucha la lista de palabras y levanta la mano si la palabra es parte de su computadora.

1. la pantalla

2. el sitio Web

3. el teclado

4. el icono

5. la dirección electrónica

6. el ratón

TELEHISTORIA ESCENA 1

Level 1 Textbook p. 359

Level 1B Textbook p. 170

TXT CD 7, Track 3

Florencia: ¡Mariano! Mira, tengo un correo electrónico de Alicia.

Mariano: ¿Qué dice, Florencia? No puedo ver la pantalla.

Florencia: Alicia quiere el autógrafo de Trini Salgado en su camiseta.

Mariano: ¡Qué bárbaro tener el autógrafo de una jugadora de fútbol famosa como Trini Salgado!

Florencia: Alicia mandó la camiseta a Sandra, una amiga que vive en Texas. Después, Sandra la mandó a un amigo de Puebla, en México, pero tampoco la encontró.

Mariano: ¿Y entonces?

Florencia: Luego, su amigo de México mandó la camiseta a Puerto Rico. Más tarde, sus amigos mandaron la camiseta a España, y entonces a Ecuador y a la República Dominicana. Y por fin, anteayer la mandaron aquí a Buenos Aires. ¡Porque Trini está aquí!

ACTIVIDAD 4 - ¿EN QUÉ ORDEN?

Level 1 Textbook p. 360

TXT CD 7, Track 4

Level 1B Textbook p. 171

Level 1B TXT CD 2, Track 2

Escucha la descripción de cómo Florencia tomó fotos y se las mandó a sus amigas. Luego indica el orden correcto de los dibujos.

El año pasado compré una cámara digital. La semana pasada tomé fotos de mis amigas en una fiesta. Anteayer quemé un disco compacto con las fotos. Anoche busqué las direcciones electrónicas de mis amigas. Hoy conecté a Internet. Por fin mandé las fotos por correo electrónico.

PRONUNCIACIÓN

Level 1 Textbook p. 363

Level 1B Textbook p. 174

TXT CD 7, Track 5

La combinación q u

You already know that c before **a**, **o**, **u**, and consonants makes the sound of the English k. To make this sound before e and i in Spanish, use **q u**/

Listen and repeat.

que

queso

pequeño

raqueta

quemar

qui

tranquilo

quince

quiero

equipo

¿Quién tiene que hacer los quehaceres?

¿Quieres ir al parque?

TELEHISTORIA ESCENA 2

Level 1 Textbook p. 364

Level 1B Textbook p. 176

TXT CD 7, Track 6

Mariano: Florencia, ¿ahora qué va a pasar con la camiseta de Alicia?

Florencia: Anoche cuando volví a casa, recibí otro correo electrónico de Alicia. Aquí está. Compartimos muchas ideas anoche. Escribió que debemos buscar a Trini en el estadio.

Mariano: Pero, ¿cuándo?

Florencia: No sé. No recibí mucha información. Tenemos que navegar por Internet para buscar la fecha y la hora. ¿Salimos para el cibercafé?

TELEHISTORIA COMPLETA

Level 1 Textbook p. 369

Level 1B Textbook p. 182

TXT CD 7, Track 7

Escena 1 - Resumen

Florencia recibe un correo electrónico de Alicia porque Trini Salgado va a estar en Buenos Aires. Sus amigos mandan la camiseta a Florencia.

Escena 2 - Resumen

Alicia escribe que Trini va a estar en el estadio. Pero Florencia y Mariano tienen que navegar por Internet para buscar más información.

Audio Scripts

Escena 3

Florencia: ¡Señor, por favor! ¿Tiene usted mi cámara?

Camarero: Sí, sí, tranquila. Aquí está. ¿Qué pasa? ¿Necesitan algo?

Mariano: No, nada. Gracias. Queremos ir al estadio para ver a Trini Salgado, pero no sabemos ni la fecha ni la hora. Nadie sabe cuándo va a llegar ella.

Florencia: Usted tampoco sabe, ¿no?

Camarero: No sé nada del estadio, pero sé que Trini Salgado va a estar en el Parque de la Costa en El Tigre, el sábado.

Florencia: ¿Sí? ¿Cómo lo sabe?

Camarero: Mira, allí dice.

Mariano: ¡Florencia! Nadie encontró a Trini… ni en Estados Unidos… ni en Puerto Rico… tampoco en España. Pero ahora, tú vas a tener el autógrafo.

ACTIVIDAD 19 (23) INTEGRACIÓN

Level 1 Textbook p. 371

TXT CD 7, Track 9

Level 1B Textbook p. 184

Level 1B TXT CD 2, Track 3

Lee la página Web y escucha el programa de radio. Explica a qué lugar prefieres ir después de las clases y por qué.

Listen and take notes

¿Qué lugar buscó Raquel? ¿Qué hay allí?

¿Qué pasó allí?

FUENTE 2

TXT CD 7, Track 9

Level 1B TXT CD 2, Track 4

¡Hola! Soy yo, Raquel Cabrera. Ayer busqué un cibercafé y encontré el Cibercafé Ratoncito. Tienen 25 computadoras nuevas y todas tienen conexión a Internet. Primero usé el mensajero instantáneo. Luego abrí el correo electrónico. ¡Alguien me mandó fotos! Abrí el mensaje, pero nunca vi las fotos. En el cibercafé no hay nadie para ayudar con el correo. Y la tarea… Es difícil pensar allí

porque muchas personas hablan por teléfono. Más tarde, comí pizza. En total, pagué nueve pesos. Para pasar una tarde divertida, el Cibercafé Ratoncito es el lugar perfecto.

LECTURA: UN CUESTIONARIO SOBRE LAS COMPUTADORAS

Level 1 Textbook pp. 372-373

Level 1B Textbook pp. 186-187

TXT CD 7, Track 10

Cuestionario: Protección para tu PC

¿Qué pasa cuando un virus infecta tu computadora? El virus funciona como un borrador. Puede destruir tus archivos. Puede afectar tu acceso a Internet y el sistema del correo electrónico. Otras personas pueden ver tus datos personales. ¿Conoces las medidas básicas que debes tomar como protección contra los virus? Toma este cuestionario para saber.

1. ¿Cuál de los siguientes no es un método típico de propagación de los virus?

A. programas que se descargan de Internet

B. archivos adjuntos a correos electrónicos

C. la provisión de datos personales en un sitio Web no seguro

D. software pirata

2. Cierto o falso: Después de instalar software antivirus, la computadora está completamente protegida.

A. cierto

B. falso

3. ¿Qué es un firewall de Internet?

A. una contraseña segura

B. un artículo de asbesto que protege la computadora de las llamas

C. un candado que puedes poner en la computadora para impedir acceso no autorizado

D. software o hardware que ayuda a proteger la computadora contra ataques como los virus

Respuestas correctas:

1. C: la provisión de datos personales en un sitio Web no seguro

2. B: falso

3. D: software o hardware que ayuda a proteger la computadora contra ataques como los virus

REPASO: ACTIVIDAD 1 - LISTEN, UNDERSTAND

Level 1 Textbook p. 376

TXT CD 7, Track 11

Level 1B Textbook p. 190

Level 1B TXT CD 2, Track 5

Diana habla con Ramiro sobre su computadora. Escucha y escribe si las oraciones son ciertas o falsas.

Ramiro: ¿Piensas que hay algún problema con tu computadora?

Diana: Sí. No recibí ningún correo electrónico ayer. No recibí nada.

Ramiro: ¿Y siempre recibes algo?

Diana: Sí. Mis amigos y yo siempre usamos Internet para mandar mensajes y fotos. También usamos el mensajero instantáneo. Pero ayer no recibí ni un correo electrónico ni una foto. Nada.

Ramiro: ¿Qué hiciste anteayer?

Diana: Anteayer yo quemé algunos discos compactos y navegué por Internet.

Ramiro: Pues, yo no encuentro ningún problema con la computadora. Tal vez tus amigos están ocupados con otras actividades.

WORKBOOK SCRIPTS
WB CD 4

INTEGRACIÓN HABLAR

Level 1 Workbook p. 304

Level 1B Workbook p. 108

WB CD 4, Track 1

Listen to the message Luis left on Guillermo's voicemail.

FUENTE 2

WB CD 4, Track 2

¡Hola, Guillermo! Soy Luis. Yo no recibí tu correo electrónico con las fotos. Nuestra amiga Andrea dice que recibió tus fotos y que son buenas. Quiero verlas pero tengo

Audio Scripts

problemas con su correo electrónico. No entiendo. Puedo navegar por el Internet en casa, pero no puedo ver mi correo electrónico. ¿Podemos hacer otra cosa para ver las fotos? Llámame. Hasta luego.

INTEGRACIÓN ESCRIBIR
Level 1 Workbook p. 305
Level 1B Workbook p. 109
WB CD 4, Track 3

Listen to Soledad's message to a customer service department. Take notes.

FUENTE 2
WB CD 4, Track 4

¡Hola! Me llamo Soledad y me encanta mi cámara nueva. Pero quiero mandar unas fotos por correo electrónico y no puedo. Encontré su sitio Web y pienso que hago todo lo que es necesario. Primero, me conecto a Internet y escribo mi dirección electrónica. Luego, hago clic en el icono para poner en el correo electrónico las fotos de mi computadora. Por fin, las mando y nunca llegan. ¿Hay algo más que necesito hacer?

ESCUCHAR A, ACTIVIDAD 1
Level 1 Workbook p. 306
Level 1B Workbook p. 110
WB CD 4, Track 5

Listen to Viviana. Then, read each sentence below and answer **cierto** (true) or **falso** (false).

Mi nombre es Viviana. El mes pasado, mi familia compró una casa en otra ciudad. Ayer tomé muchas fotos con mi cámara digital: tomé fotos de los parques, tomé fotos de mis amigos nuevos y tomé fotos de las casas. No tomé ninguna más porque quiero mandar las fotos ahora. Hoy les mando todas las fotos a mis amigos de la escuela. Creo que van a gustarles.

ESCUCHAR A, ACTIVIDAD 2
Level 1 Workbook p. 306

Level 1B Workbook p. 110
WB CD 4, Track 6

Listen to Julio. Then, complete the sentences.

Mi amiga Viviana me mandó unas fotos fantásticas. Las tomó con la cámara digital que recibió como regalo de cumpleaños. Algunos de sus amigos le regalaron esa cámara. Ella puede mandarnos las fotos de su casa nueva. Cuando ella nos escribe un correo electrónico, nos manda fotos o hablamos por el mensajero instantáneo. Entonces estamos cerca de ella.

ESCUCHAR B, ACTIVIDAD 1
Level 1 Workbook p. 307
Level 1B Workbook p. 111
WB CD 4, Track 7

Listen to Sebastián and take notes. Then, draw a line between the people and the photos they take.

Me llamo Sebastián. Mis amigos y yo tomamos muchas fotos. Nos gusta mucho. Silvana toma fotos de los parques. A Nicolás le gusta tomar fotos de casas viejas. A mí me encanta tomar fotos de personas. Pedro toma fotos de coches y autobuses. A él le gusta eso, yo no sé por qué. Miriam toma fotos del mar y la playa. Anteayer, mandamos las fotos a un sitio web; allí van a salir algunas fotos. Vimos ese sitio el mes pasado y nos gustó la idea.

ESCUCHAR B, ACTIVIDAD 2
Level 1 Workbook p. 307
Level 1B Workbook p. 111
WB CD 4, Track 8

Listen to the conversation between Pedro and Silvana. Take notes. Then, complete the following sentences.

Silvana: Hola, Pedro. ¿Mandaste las fotos al sitio web que encontramos?

Pedro: No. A nadie le gustan mis fotos.

Silvana: ¿Por qué? Tú tomas muy buenas fotos.

Pedro: Pero nadie quiere fotos ni de coches ni de autobuses.

Silvana: ¡No es verdad! ¿Recibiste las fotos que te mandé anteayer? Son de un chico que toma fotos de esas cosas. ¡Y ganó un premio el año pasado!

Pedro: Sí, pero no pienso que alguien puede ganar un premio por eso.

ESCUCHAR C, ACTIVIDAD 1
Level 1 Workbook p. 308
Level 1B Workbook p. 112
WB CD 4, Track 9

Listen to Armando and take notes. Then complete the following table with the information.

Hola, soy Armando. Hoy es el cumpleaños de mi hijo, Diego. Quiero regalarle una computadora nueva. A él le encanta navegar en Internet. Su tío quiere regalarle una cámara digital porque le gusta tomar fotos y mandarlas a sus amigos. Su hermano vio la semana pasada un tocadiscos compactos y quiere comprarlo. A Diego le encanta escuchar música. La computadora nueva también tiene que servir para quemar discos compactos.

ESCUCHAR C, ACTIVIDAD 2
Level 1 Workbook p. 308
Level 1B Workbook p. 112
WB CD 4, Track 10

Listen to the conversation between Javier and Sandra. Take notes. Then, answer the following questions.

Javier: ¡Sandra!, ¿viste el tocadiscos compactos que le compré a Diego?

Sandra: ¡Qué lindo, Javier! Diego tiene muchos regalos este año. Mi papá le compró una cámara digital.

Javier: ¡Fantástico! Le compramos muchos regalos porque el año pasado no recibió ninguno. Él vivió un año en la casa de mi abuela y la casa de mi abuela está muy lejos.

Sandra: Sí, yo sé. ¿Tú no viviste también en la casa de tu abuela?

Javier: Sí, yo viví ocho meses con mi abuela. Ella está enferma y alguien siempre tiene que estar con ella. No puede estar sola.

Audio Scripts

Sandra: ¡Qué buenos chicos! Diego tiene que recibir muchos regalos. ¡Y tú también!

Javier: Pero mi cumpleaños es el mes que viene.

ASSESSMENT SCRIPTS
TEST CD 2

LESSON 1 TEST: ESCUCHAR
ACTIVIDAD A

Modified Assessment Book p. 242
On-level Assessment Book p. 307
Pre-AP Assessment Book p. 242
TEST CD 2, Track 13

Listen to the following audio. Then complete Activity A.

En el Centro de Computadoras, necesitas saber usar una computadora. ¿Te gusta el Internet? ¿Quieres hacer un sitio Web? ¿Quieres usar tu cámara digital? Tenemos todo aquí. Las clases empiezan el lunes.

El lunes hay clases para estudiantes que no saben usar una computadora.

El martes hay clases para aprender a navegar por Internet.

El miércoles hay clases para estudiantes que quieren hacer un sitio Web.

El jueves tenemos una clase para las personas a quienes les gusta usar su cámara digital.

El viernes hay una clase para hacer música con una computadora.

¡Ven ahora al Centro de Computadoras!

ESCUCHAR ACTIVIDAD B

Modified Assessment Book p. 242
On-level Assessment Book p. 307
Pre-AP Assessment Book p. 242
TEST CD 2, Track 14

Listen to the following audio. Then complete Activity B.

Francisco: ¿Qué necesitas hacer, papá?

Padre: Bueno, quiero mandar un correo electrónico.

Francisco: Es muy fácil, papá. Aquí está la computadora. Primero, te conectas a Internet. Luego haz clic en el icono. Luego escribe la dirección electrónica y tu correo. Por fin, haz clic y manda el correo.

Padre: Ya escribí el correo, y "clic", ya lo mandé.

Francisco: ¡Papá, estás en línea! ¿Qué quieres hacer ahora? ¿Quieres navegar por Internet? ¿Quieres usar el mensajero instantáneo?

Padre: Gracias, hijo. No quiero hacer nada más. Ya aprendí mucho. Usar la computadora es muy difícil.

HERITAGE LEARNER SCRIPTS
HL CDS 2 & 4

INTEGRACIÓN HABLAR

Level 1 HL Workbook p. 306
Level 1B HL Workbook p. 110
HL CD 2, Track 17

Escucha un anuncio de radio. Puedes tomar notas mientras escuchas y luego responde a las preguntas.

INTEGRACIÓN HABLAR

HL CD 2, Track 18

¿No entiende usted de computadoras? ¿Alguien le pregunta si está en línea y usted inmediatamente piensa en el supermercado? El Instituto Computacional Ulises anuncia el período de matrículas. Los cursos de Internet para principiantes y para avanzados constan de cuatro sesiones. Las clases son los viernes y los sábados por la mañana. Cada clase dura tres horas. Con la cuota de inscripción tiene usted acceso a nuestro laboratorio de computadoras abierto las 24 horas. No lo piense más. Inscríbase hoy mismo. Llame al 20-34-33 y reserve su lugar. 20-34-33 y sea parte de la modernidad.

INTEGRACIÓN ESCRIBIR

Level 1 HL Workbook p. 307
Level 1B HL Workbook p. 111
HL CD 2, Track 19

Ahora vas a escuchar el mensaje que Ítalo Luján dejó en el contestador de su familia. Pedes tomar notas mientras escuchas y luego realiza la actividad.

INTEGRACIÓN ESCRIBIR

HL CD 2, Track 20

Pero Raúl, ché, ¿dónde te has metido hoy? Te he enviado más de cinco correos electrónicos y no me respondes. Vos sabés que no tengo plata para la tarjeta telefónica. ¡Háblame, hermano! Los archivos que me mandaste llegaron corruptos y no he podido abrirlos. Mi presentación es mañana y no sé qué voy ha hacer si no tengo esas fotos. Por favor, no mandes los MP3 en el mismo correo. Mi conexión de Internet es malísima y me toma horas bajarlos.

HL Assessment Book p. 248
HL CD 4, Track 13

Escucha el siguiente audio. Luego, completa la actividad A.

Pepito: ¿Qué hiciste ayer, Jacobo?

Jacobo: Les mandé unas fotos a los abuelos.

Pepito: ¿Cómo las mandaste?

Jacobo: Con la computadora.

Pepito: ¿Y qué hiciste hoy?

Jacobo: Por la mañana corrí cinco kilómetros en el parque...

Pepito: ¿Y luego?

Jacobo: Y luego volví a casa y estudié toda la mañana.

Pepito: ¿Y qué hiciste después de estudiar?

Jacobo: Bajé a la cocina y almorcé.

Pepito: ¿Y qué comiste?

Jacobo: Un sándwich.

Pepito: ¿Y qué bebiste?

Jacobo: Un vaso de agua.

Pepito: ¿Y qué hiciste por la tarde?

Jacobo: Bueno... por la tarde conecté a Internet...

Audio Scripts

Pepito: ¿Y por qué conectaste a Internet?

Jacobo: Para buscar información para la clase de historia, quemar un disco compacto, preparar mi sitio Web y escribir correos electrónicos a mis amigos para saber qué hacen.

Pepito: ¿Por qué?

Jacobo: Porque para mañana todos tenemos que terminar un trabajo para la clase de

historia.

Pepito: ¿Y qué es la historia?

Jacobo: Ah, Pepito. Mañana te lo explico.

ESCUCHAR ACTIVIDAD B

HL Assessment Book p. 248

HL CD 4, Track 14

Escucha el siguiente audio. Luego, completa la actividad B.

Mis hijos me mandaron esta computadora el mes pasado y todavía no sé usarla. A ver... dicen que si hago clic en este icono puedo escribir un documento... ¿pero es este icono aquí, al pie de la página, o el icono que está encima del icono rojo? ¡Ay! No lo sé. Y quiero mandarles a mis hijos las fotos que tomé el mes pasado, durante mi fiesta de cumpleaños, pero tampoco sé cómo. Y nadie me explicó cómo usar la nueva cámara digital... Y me gustaría conectar a Internet porque quiero ver el sitio Web de nuestra hija que es una gran artista... ¡pero tampoco sé cómo! ¿Y qué hago para mandar un correo electrónico? Veo que me escribió nuestro hijo Juan, pero cómo ni sé contestarle, ni sé usar el mensajero instantáneo, voy a tener que llamarle a Juan o estudiar una clase de informática... ¡porque alguien tiene que enseñarme cómo usar esta computadora!

Audio Scripts

UNIDAD 7, LECCIÓN 2
TEXTBOOK SCRIPTS
TXT CD 7
LEVEL 1B TXT CD 2

PRESENTACIÓN DE VOCABULARIO

Level 1 Textbook pp. 380-381

Level 1B Textbook pp. 194-196

TXT CD 7, Track 12

A. Mariano: Voy a llamar a Florencia para invitarla a hacer algo este fin de semana.

B. Mariano: ¿Aló? ¿Puedo hablar con Florencia?
Florencia: Hola, Mariano. Soy yo, Florencia.
Mariano: Hola, Florencia. ¿Quieres acompañarme al zoológico? Te invito.
Florencia: Lo siento. No me gusta mucho ir al zoológico.
Mariano: ¿Te gustaría ir a la feria del libro el sábado?
Florencia: ¡Qué lástima! El sábado no puedo, pero me gustaría hacer algo el domingo.
Mariano: Voy a ir al parque de diversiones con Luciana. ¿Quieres ir?
Florencia: ¡Claro que sí! Hasta el domingo.

C. Mariano: Hola, Florencia. Hola, Luciana. Vamos a comprar los boletos. Primero quiero subir a la vuelta al mundo.

D. Mariano: No voy a subir a la montaña rusa porque tengo miedo. Luciana y yo preferimos los autitos chocadores. Son más divertidos.

¡A RESPONDER!

Level 1 Textbook p. 381

TXT CD 7, Track 13

Level 1B Textbook p. 196

Level 1B TXT CD 2, Track 6

Mariano invita a Luciana al museo. Escucha sus respuestas y señala con el pulgar hacia arriba si ella acepta la invitación o con el pulgar hacia abajo si no la acepta.

1. Me gustaría ir al museo.
2. ¡Qué lástima!
3. ¡Claro que sí!
4. Sí, me encantaría.

TELEHISTORIA ESCENA 1

Level 1 Textbook p. 383

Level 1B Textbook p. 198

TXT CD 7, Track 14

Florencia: ¿Dónde está Mariano? Tengo que llamarlo a su teléfono celular.

Mariano: Hola, Florencia. Sí, Luciana y yo estamos en el Parque de la Costa. Compramos nuestros boletos.

Florencia: Yo también. ¿Pueden ver la montaña rusa?

Mariano: Sí, pero estamos más cerca de la vuelta al mundo.

Florencia: Ahora veo la vuelta al mundo. Ustedes deben estar cerca.

Mariano: Sí, sí. Veo la montaña rusa, pero no te veo.

Luciana: ¿Por qué no encontramos a Florencia delante de los autitos chocadores?

ACTIVIDAD 7 – FUERON A DIFERENTES LUGARES

Level 1 Textbook p. 387

TXT CD 7, Track 15

Level 1B Textbook p. 201

Level 1B TXT CD 2, Track 7

Escucha las descripciones y contesta las preguntas.

Soy Florencia. Fui al parque de diversiones con mi amiga. Subimos a la montaña rusa pero no me gustó. Tengo miedo de las montañas rusas. ¡Fue horrible!

Me llamo Luciana. Mi hermano y yo fuimos a la feria del libro. Compré tres libros nuevos. ¡Qué interesante!

Soy Mariano. Florencia me invitó al museo. Pasamos todo el día allí. Vimos un Picasso. Nos gustó mucho. ¡Qué divertido!

TELEHISTORIA ESCENA 2

Level 1 Textbook p. 388

Level 1B Textbook p. 204

TXT CD 7, Track 16

Luciana: ¡Ay! Che, Mariano, ¿adónde fuiste?

Mariano: Yo fui a ver dónde podemos encontrar a Trini. Sé dónde está.

Luciana: ¿Cómo lo sabes?

Mariano: Fue el señor de la ventanilla. Él dice que Trini fue a la vuelta al mundo.

Florencia: Mariano, ¡qué bárbaro! ¡Vamos!

Florencia: El señor dice que Trini y sus amigos fueron a comer.

Mariano: ¿Trini fue a comer? ¡Ay, no! ¿Qué podemos hacer? Tenemos que ir a buscarla.

Luciana: Fuimos a la vuelta al mundo, fuimos al restaurante. ¿Dónde está Trini? Nunca la vamos a encontrar.

PRONUNCIACIÓN

Level 1 Textbook p. 389

Level 1B Textbook p. 205

TXT CD 7, Track 17

Las letras Y y LL

The letter combination **ll** <"elle"> in Spanish sounds like the English y in yet. The **y** has the same sound unless it stands alone or is at the end of a word, in which case the y is pronounced like the ee in the English word see.

Listen and repeat.

llamar
tobillo
rodilla
ella
galleta
yo
ayer
playa
mayo
desayuno
y
hay
muy
hoy

Yo me **ll**amo Marco **y** ella es **Y**olanda.

Hoy voy a la playa de Marbella. Es muy bonita.

TELEHISTORIA COMPLETA

Level 1 Textbook p. 393

Level 1B Textbook p. 210

TXT CD 7, Track 18

Escena 1 – Resumen

Florencia va al parque de diversiones para buscar a Trini Salgado, pero primero necesita encontrar a Mariano y a su amiga, Luciana.

Escena 2 – Resumen

Los amigos van a la vuelta al mundo y al restaurante para buscar a Trini Salgado, pero no la encuentran.

Audio Scripts

Escena 3

Luciana: Empanadas, ¡qué ricas! Voy a comprar unas.

Florencia: Gracias, Luciana. ¿Por qué no compras un refresco para mí, y unas empanadas para nosotros dos? Y Mariano, ¿te gustaría venir conmigo a buscar a Trini a los autitos chocadores?

Manager: «Atención, por favor, señorita Trini Salgado, por favor, la esperan en la puerta, señorita Trini Salgado».

Florencia y Mariano: ¡Vamos!

Mujer: Señor, ¡yo soy Trini Salgado!

Florencia: ¿Trini Salgado? ¿La jugadora de fútbol?

Mujer: ¿La jugadora de fútbol?

ACTIVIDAD 18 (22) - INTEGRACIÓN

Level 1 Textbook p. 395

TXT CD 7, Track 19

Level 1B Textbook p. 212

Level 1B TXT CD 2, Track 8

Lee la nota y escucha el mensaje telefónico. Decide qué invitación quieres aceptar, y deja un mensaje para Álvaro y después para Carlos para decirles si vas a ir o no.

FUENTE 2

TXT CD 7, Track 20

Level 1B TXT CD 2, Track 9

Listen and take notes

¿Qué hizo Carlos anteayer?

¿Qué quiere hacer mañana? ¿Cuál es el problema?

Hola. Soy yo, Carlos. Si no tienes planes para mañana a la una y media, tengo una idea. Escucha: anteayer fui al estadio de fútbol. Compré boletos para el partido; un boleto para mi hermana y uno para mí. Pagué 50 pesos por los dos boletos. Es mucho dinero, pero las sillas están muy cerca del campo. Ahora tengo un problema... ¡mi hermana está enferma! Ella no puede ir conmigo. ¿Quieres acompañarme tú? Puedes pagarme los 25 pesos después. Llámame al teléfono celular. Adiós.

LECTURA: MUSEOS EXCEPCIONALES

Level 1 Textbook pp. 396-397

Level 1B Textbook pp. 214-215

TXT CD 7, Track 21

¿Qué imaginas cuando piensas en un museo? Muchas personas imaginan cuartos formales con obras de arte.

Hay museos en Latinoamérica que celebran su cultura y también dan una experiencia diferente, sin tantas restricciones como un museo tradicional.

El Museo al Aire Libre no tiene ni puertas ni paredes, pero es uno de los museos más populares de Buenos Aires. Está en el corazón de La Boca, una sección de Buenos Aires cerca del mar, en una calle pequeña que se llama el Caminito. Allí viven muchos artistas argentinos en sus famosas casas multicolores.

El Caminito sirve como un marco natural para diversas obras de arte: pinturas, esculturas y murales. Es posible caminar por la calle, ver obras de arte, comer en cafés, escuchar música y mirar a personas que bailan el tango.

La cultura boliviana, especialmente la música, tiene dos orígenes: indígena y español. En el centro de La Paz, Bolivia, la calle Jaén tiene varios museos de arte donde puedes ver obras indígenas. El Museo de Instrumentos Musicales es un poco diferente de los otros. En este museo interactivo, ¡puedes tocar algunos de los instrumentos! Allí hay exhibiciones de instrumentos precolombinos, instrumentos de viento y tambores. Puedes tocar instrumentos como el charango, una guitarra pequeña de influencia española.

REPASO: ACTIVIDAD 1 – LISTEN AND UNDERSTAND

Level 1 Textbook p. 400

TXT CD 7, Track 22

Level 1B Textbook p. 252

Level 1B TXT CD 2, Track 10

Escucha las conversaciones. En una hoja de papel, escribe sí si el invitado o la invitada acepta la invitación, o no si no la acepta.

1. ¿Quieres acompañarme al museo el sábado?

Lo siento. Fui al museo anteayer y fue un poco aburrido.

2. ¿Te gustaría ir al zoológico conmigo?

Sí, me encantaría ir al zoológico. ¿A qué hora salimos?

3. Voy a la feria el viernes. ¿Quieres acompañarme?

¿La feria? ¡Qué divertido! Hasta el viernes.

4. Tengo dos boletos para ir al acuario el domingo. Te invito.

¡Qué lástima! Voy a salir con mi familia el domingo.

5. ¿Quieres hacer algo este fin de semana?

¡Claro que sí! ¿Adónde vamos?

6. Fui al parque de diversiones anoche. La montaña rusa fue muy divertida. Voy a volver hoy. ¿Te gustaría ir conmigo?

¿La montaña rusa? ¡Qué miedo! Prefiero ir al zoológico.

COMPARACIÓN CULTURAL: ¿CONOCES UN LUGAR DIVERTIDO?

Level 1 Textbook pp. 402-403

Level 1B Textbook pp. 220-221

TXT CD 7, Track 23

Bolivia, Luis.

Luis: ¿Qué tal? Soy Luis y vivo en La Paz, en las montañas de los Andes. Anteayer mis amigos y yo hicimos algo divertido. Primero fuimos al Paseo el Prado, una calle divertida. Allí caminamos y miramos los restaurantes y las tiendas. Por fin llegamos a la Plaza del Estudiante. Encontramos a otros amigos allí. Hizo buen tiempo, entonces hablamos y paseamos en la plaza. ¡Qué bonito!

Argentina, Liliana.

Liliana: ¡Hola! Me llamo Liliana y soy de Buenos Aires. Ayer mi hermana y yo fuimos a un parque de diversiones cerca de mi casa. Primero nosotras subimos a la montaña rusa, pero a mí no me gustó. ¡Qué miedo! Me gustaron más los autitos chocadores. Más tarde comimos unas hamburguesas. Luego miramos un espectáculo de láser. Volvimos a casa en la noche, cuando cerró el parque. ¡Qué bárbaro!

Nicaragua, Eva.

Eva: Me llamo Eva y soy de Managua. El jueves pasado mis padres y yo fuimos a Masaya, el centro folklórico de Nicaragua. Todos los jueves, en el Mercado Nacional de Artesanías celebran las Verbenas de Masaya: un festival folklórico de danza y música. Los artistas llevan trajes de muchos colores. ¡Tomé unas fotos fabulosas! Después compramos artesanías y comimos comidas típicas de Nicaragua. ¡Fue muy divertido!

REPASO: ACTIVIDAD 1 – LISTEN, UNDERSTAND AND COMPARE

Level 1 Textbook p. 404

Level 1B Textbook p. 222

TXT CD 7, Track 24

Audio Scripts

Listen to the phone conversation. Then, answer the following questions.

Sra. Palomar: ¿Aló?

Teresa: Buenas tardes. ¿Puedo hablar con Jaime?

Sra. Palomar: ¿Quién habla?

Teresa: Perdón... habla Teresa, Teresa Rodríguez. Soy una amiga de Jaime.

Sra. Palomar: Ah, claro... ¡Teresa! Soy la madrastra de Jaime. Lo siento, pero él no está aquí en casa. Salió al parque. Fue con unos amigos. ¿Quieres dejar un mensaje?

Teresa: No, gracias. Quiero ir a la feria con él pero yo...

Sra. Palomar: O, si quieres hablar con él ahora, puedes llamarlo a su teléfono celular.

Teresa: Muy bien. El número es 335-9064, ¿no?

Sra. Palomar: No, no. Es 335-9074.

Teresa: Muchas gracias, señora Palomar.

Sra. Palomar: Adiós.

WORKBOOK SCRIPTS
WB CD 4

INTEGRACIÓN HABLAR

Level 1 Workbook p. 327

Level 1B Workbook p. 131

WB CD 4, Track 11

Listen to Cecilia's message on Alejandra's cell phone. Take notes.

FUENTE 2

WB CD 4, Track 12

¡Hola, Alejandra! Recibí tu invitación y me encantaría ir. Pero no por la tarde, porque por la tarde, ¡qué lástima! no tengo tiempo. Podemos ir al lugar que dices temprano. También me gustaría cenar en el Restaurante Sol por la noche. Las pizzas allí son muy ricas y también tienen otros platos principales que me gustan. Entonces, ¡claro que sí! Nos vemos el sábado.

INTEGRACIÓN ESCRIBIR

Level 1 Workbook p. 328

Level 1B Workbook p. 132

WB CD 4, Track 13

Listen to the explanations given through loudspeakers in the museum. Take notes.

FUENTE 2

WB CD 4, Track 14

El bate que está cerca de la puerta, fue de un gran jugador. Él ganó el campeonato con este bate en 1987. Al lado del bate, está el premio y un casco rojo que también eran de él. Si nos acompañan por aquí, cerca de la ventana, pueden ver una camiseta que fue de otro gran jugador y, si suben las escaleras, pueden ver su guante.

ESCUCHAR A, ACTIVIDAD 1

Level 1 Workbook p. 329

Level 1B Workbook p. 133

WB CD 4, Track 15

Listen to Federico. Then, place an "x" next to the sentences that describe what happened.

Hola, me llamo Federico. El fin de semana pasado, mis amigos y yo fuimos al parque de diversiones. Todos subimos a la vuelta al mundo pero Susana no subió; ella tiene miedo de los lugares muy altos. Todos hablamos con ella pero ella no subió. Después fuimos a los autitos chocadores. Esta vez, todos subimos. ¡Fue divertido!

ESCUCHAR A, ACTIVIDAD 2

Level 1 Workbook p. 329

Level 1B Workbook p. 133

WB CD 4, Track 16

Listen to Susana. Then, complete the sentences.

Hola, soy Susana. Cuando fui al parque de diversiones con mis amigos, ellos hicieron algunas cosas que yo no hice porque tengo miedo. Es que yo tengo miedo de subir a algunos juegos. Creo que la vuelta al mundo es un juego peligroso. Mis amigos hablaron conmigo pero no subí. Después del parque de diversiones, fuimos a escuchar música a la casa de Noemí. Lo pasamos muy bien.

ESCUCHAR B, ACTIVIDAD 1

Level 1 Workbook p. 330

Level 1B Workbook p. 134

WB CD 4, Track 17

Listen to Teresa and take notes. Then, underline the word that completes each sentence.

Soy Teresa y ayer invité a Jaime a ir al zoológico. Me gusta ir con él porque sabe mucho de todos los animales. El año pasado, en la clase de ciencias, siempre sacó buenas notas. Hoy llegamos temprano al zoológico y fuimos a ver todos los animales. El zoológico es muy grande y caminamos mucho. Aprendí de los animales y los lugares donde viven. ¡Qué interesante!

ESCUCHAR B, ACTIVIDAD 2

Level 1 Workbook p. 330

Level 1B Workbook p. 134

WB CD 4, Track 18

Listen to Jaime and take notes. Then, complete the table below with the information requested.

Me llamo Jaime y hoy fui al zoológico con Teresa. Ella compró el boleto para ella y para mí. Fue muy buena amiga. A mí me encanta ir al zoológico porque me gustan mucho los animales. El año pasado recibí un libro de los zoológicos de todos los países. Mi papá lo compró para él y después de leerlo pensó en mí. Entonces me lo regaló. Él sabe que me gustan los animales. También, el mes pasado, mi mamá me regaló un libro con fotos de todos los animales. Fue el mejor regalo.

ESCUCHAR C, ACTIVIDAD 1

Level 1 Workbook p. 331

Level 1B Workbook p. 135

WB CD 4, Track 19

Listen to Luis. Then, write four things that happened in Catalina's house and four things that happened in the movie.

Soy Luis. El fin de semana pasado fue muy divertido. Mis amigos y yo vimos una película en la casa de Catalina. Fueron todos los chicos de la clase. La película es de un chico que conoce a una chica en una playa. Van a un parque de diversiones y a la chica le gusta estar con él. Pero los padres de la chica los ven en la vuelta al mundo. Los padres de ella no quieren al chico. La película es triste pero termina bien. Catalina preparó unos sándwiches y Ramón compró unos refrescos. Después escuchamos música y tocamos la guitarra.

ESCUCHAR C, ACTIVIDAD 2

Level 1 Workbook p. 331

Level 1B Workbook p. 135

WB CD 4, Track 20

Listen to Catalina's conversation and take notes. Then, answer the following questions.

Audio Scripts

Buenas tardes. Me llamo Catalina. Este fin de semana mis amigos y yo vimos una película en mi casa. Lo pasamos muy bien. Después de ver la película, algunos chicos fueron a comprar refrescos y cosas ricas. Manuel tiene unos discos compactos de música rock y todos bailamos y cantamos. A Luis le gusta María. Él tiene una guitarra y tocó música para ella. Me gusta recibir a mis amigos en casa... ¡me encantó lo que hicimos.

ASSESSMENT SCRIPTS
TEST CD 2

LESSON 2 TEST: ESCUCHAR
ACTIVIDAD A

Modified Assessment Book p. 254

On-level Assessment Book p. 324

Pre-AP Assessment Book p. 254

TEST CD 2, Track 15

Listen to the following audio. Then complete Activity A.

Señora Flores: ¿Aló?

Daniel: Buenos días, Señora. ¿Está Miguel, por favor?

Señora Flores: Daniel, ¿eres tú?

Daniel: Sí, Señora.

Señora Flores: Lo siento, Daniel. Miguel no está en casa. Fue al museo de historia con su padre.

Daniel: ¡Qué divertido! ¿Puedo dejar un mensaje?

Señora Flores: Claro que sí. Un momento. Necesito un papel y un lápiz.

Daniel: Hay una fiesta en mi casa el sábado a las ocho y quiero invitar a Miguel.

Señora Flores: Muy bien. . . una fiesta. . . el sábado. . . a las ocho…

Daniel: Muchas gracias, Señora.

ACTIVIDAD B

Modified Assessment Book p. 254

On-level Assessment Book p. 324

Pre-AP Assessment Book p. 254

TEST CD 2, Track 16

Listen to the following audio. Then complete Activity B.

Mi familia y yo fuimos al parque de diversiones. Primero, subí a la montaña rusa con mi hermano mayor. ¡Qué miedo! ¡Pero, me gustó muchísimo! Después fui a los autitos chocadores con mi padre. Entonces, toda la familia subió a la vuelta al mundo. ¡Qué bonita!

Luego, compramos hamburguesas, papas fritas y jugos. En la noche, compramos boletos para el teatro. Hay un teatro muy grande en el parque de diversiones. ¡Qué día divertido!

UNIT 7 TEST: ESCUCHAR
ACTIVIDAD A

Modified Assessment Book p. 266

On-level Assessment Book p. 336

Pre-AP Assessment Book p. 266

TEST CD 2, Track 17

Listen to the following audio. Then complete Activity A.

Ayer pasé el día en mi casa. Fue un día muy ocupado porque trabajé todo el día en la computadora. Primero, me conecté a Internet y usé el mensajero instantáneo con mi amigo que vive en California. Entonces, quemé un disco compacto con las fotos digitales que tomé cuando fui a México el año pasado. Luego, mandé unos correos electrónicos a mis amigos. Más tarde, hice la tarea para la escuela. Cuando terminé la tarea, hice un clic en un icono para abrir mi sitio Web favorito. Por fin, llamé a mis primos pero nadie contestó y dejé un mensaje.

ACTIVIDAD B

Modified Assessment Book p. 266

On-level Assessment Book p. 336

Pre-AP Assessment Book p. 266

TEST CD 2, Track 18

Listen to the following audio. Then complete Activity B.

Leo: Hola, Sandra, ¿cómo fue tu fin de semana?

Sandra: Ah, fue muy divertido.

Leo: ¿Qué hiciste?

Sandra: Bueno, el sábado fui a la feria en el centro con mi prima.

Leo: ¡Qué divertido! ¿Qué compraste?

Sandra: No compré nada pero comimos helado en la feria. Entonces, hablé con mis abuelos en mi teléfono celular y nos invitaron al zoológico.

Leo: ¿Fueron al zoológico?

Sandra: ¡Claro que sí!

Leo: ¿Tomaron fotos?

Sandra: Sí, tomamos algunas fotos muy bonitas.

Leo: ¿Qué hiciste el domingo?

Sandra: Fuimos al acuario y cuando salimos del acuario, fuimos al nuevo museo de arte.

Leo: Hicieron muchas cosas.

Sandra: Bueno, mis abuelos nunca descansan. Siempre quieren hacer algo.

Leo: ¿A qué hora volvieron a casa?

Sandra: Fuimos a casa a las seis de la tarde.

Leo: ¿Estás muy cansada o quieres acompañarme al cine? Te invito.

Sandra: Sí, me encantaría.

HERITAGE LEARNERS SCRIPTS
HL CDS 2 & 4

INTEGRACIÓN HABLAR

Level 1 HL Workbook p. 329

Level 1B HL Workbook p. 133

HL CD 2, Track 21

Escucha el siguiente audio. Puedes tomar nota mientras escuchas y luego responde a las preguntas

FUENTE 2

HL CD 2, Track 22

A Felipe le encantan las atracciones mecánicas, especialmente las montañas rusas. Creo que ese es un buen lugar para celebrarle su cumpleaños. Mi amiga Juanita me dijo que hace poco abrieron un parque de diversiones a la salida de la ciudad. Dice que el parque tiene una vuelta al mundo enorme. El problema es que las entradas son muy costosas y este mes estoy un poco pobre. Espero que podamos ir porque Felipe es un buen amigo.

INTEGRACIÓN ESCRIBIR

Level 1 HL Workbook p. 330

Level 1B HL Workbook p. 134

HL CD 2, Track 23

Escucha el siguiente anuncio de radio. Puedes tomar notas mientras escuchas y luego completa la actividad.

FUENTE 2

HL CD 2, Track 24

El Parque Central, su parque de atracciones favorito, lanza su primera convocatoria del año. ¿Tienes creatividad? ¿Qué tanto sabes de piratas? Escribe una biografía de nuestro personaje principal en la Gruta del Terror, Barba Azul. ¿De

Audio Scripts

dónde viene? ¿Qué hizo? ¿Cuántas batallas ganó? ¿Cómo perdió el ojo izquierdo? La mejor biografía recibirá un pasaporte anual para el escritor y su familia completamente gratis. También tendrá una cena para él o ella y diez de sus mejores amigos en el nuevo restaurante «El Tesoro de Barba Azul». Manda tu biografía antes del 10 de abril.

LESSON 2 TEST: ESCUCHAR
ACTIVIDAD A

HL Assessment Book p. 260

HL CD 4, Track 15

Escucha el siguiente audio. Luego, completa la Actividad A.

Luis: Ana, ¿subimos a la montaña rusa? Es muy divertida. Estamos al lado de ella.

Ana: Tal vez, más tarde... ahora no.

Luis: Bueno... ¿qué tal si subimos a la vuelta al mundo? Está muy cerca. Mira, aquí está.

Ana: ¡Ay, no! Es tan alta. ¡Qué miedo!

Luis: Pero no es peligroso subir. La semana pasada subió mi hermanito que tiene sólo seis años y mi abuelo, que tiene setenta.

Ana: Bueno... creo que va a ser más divertido subir a los autitos chocadores, ¿no?

Luis: ¡No! Los autitos chocadores son para los pequeños. ¡Qué aburridos son!

Ana: Mira, Luis, si tú subes conmigo a los autitos chocadores, luego subo a la vuelta al mundo contigo.

Luis: Bueno... ¿y después subimos a la montaña rusa?

Ana: Vamos a ver... tengo mucho miedo y me parece peligroso... ¿por qué no visitamos el acuario que está aquí también?

Luis: Bueno... voy al acuario contigo si luego subes conmigo a la montaña rusa... infantil, ¿vale?

Ana: ¡Muy bien, Luis!

LESSON 2 TEST: ESCUCHAR
ACTIVIDAD B

HL Assessment Book p. 260

HL CD 4, Track 16

Escucha el siguiente audio. Luego, completa la actividad B.

Claudia: ¿Aló?

José: ¿Claudia?

Claudia: Sí.

José: Soy José. ¿Qué tal?

Claudia: Muy bien. ¿Cómo estás?

José: Bien, gracias. Oye, Claudia, me gustaría invitarte al museo el viernes.

Claudia: Lo siento, José. El viernes no puedo. Tengo que ir a casa de mis abuelos.

José: ¿Quieres acompañarme a la feria del libro? Es el sábado.

Claudia: ¡Qué lástima! El sábado tengo clases de guitarra y baile. No puedo.

José: Bueno... ¿Y qué tal por la noche? Podemos ir al cine. Ponen la última película de Almodóvar.

Claudia: Lo siento. Pero fui al cine ayer y vi esta película. No me gustó.

José: ¿Y el domingo? Podemos ir al acuario. Y te invito a cenar después.

Claudia: Sí, me encantaría. ¿A qué hora quieres ir?

José: ¿Está bien a las dos?

Claudia: ¡Claro que sí! ¡Hasta el domingo!

José: ¡Hasta el domingo!

UNIT 7 TEST: ESCUCHAR
ACTIVIDAD A

HL Assessment Book p. 272

HL CD 4, Track 17

Escucha el siguiente audio. Luego, completa la Actividad A.

Beatriz: ¿Aló?

Arturo: ¿Hola, Beatriz. ¿Cómo estás? Soy Arturo.

Beatriz: Más o menos. Ayer salí con Ana y no volví a casa hasta muy tarde. Hoy estoy un poco cansada.

Arturo: ¿Qué hicieron ustedes?

Beatriz: Hicimos muchas cosas. Primero fuimos de compras y luego fuimos un rato a la feria del libro. Fue muy interesante. Después fuimos al zoológico y luego comimos en un café que está al lado del zoológico. Más tarde fui con Ana al nuevo museo de arte porque ayer lo abrieron por la tarde.

Arturo: ¿Y luego?

Beatriz: Luego fuimos a la fiesta de cumpleaños del hermano de Ana. Fue una fiesta muy divertida.

Arturo: ¿Y dónde fue la fiesta?

Beatriz: En el nuevo restaurante argentino, ¿lo conoces?

Arturo: Sí, es muy bueno. Fui allí la semana pasada.

Beatriz: Pero anoche no volví a casa hasta la una de la mañana. Por eso estoy cansada.

Arturo: Pero no tan cansada para no salir otra vez esta noche, ¿verdad?

Beatriz: Bueno...

Arturo: Es que... ¿quieres acompañarme al cibercafé para hacer un sitio Web? Entiendes las computadoras tan bien...

Beatriz: Lo siento, Arturo, pero anoche no hice la tarea y mañana tenemos examen.

Arturo: ¡Qué lástima!

Beatriz: Sí, pero me gustaría acompañarte otro día.

UNIT 7 TEST: ESCUCHAR
ACTIVIDAD B

HL Assessment Book p. 272

HL CD 4, Track 18

Escucha el siguiente audio. Luego, completa la Actividad B.

Germán: Buenos días.

Luisa: Buenos días. ¿Está Isabel, por favor?

Germán: No, no está.

Luisa: ¿Puedo dejarle un mensaje?

Germán: ¡Claro que sí!

Luisa: Por favor, dile que llamó su amiga Luisa.

Germán: ...su amiga Luisa.

Luisa: Sí, y dile que voy a ir a la feria del libro a las tres de la tarde con dos amigos: Javier y Alejandro.

Germán: ...Javier y Alejandro.

Luisa: Sí, son los estudiantes nuevos. Isabel no los conoce pero los va a conocer esta tarde. Ella debe estar en la feria del libro a las tres.

Germán: ...a las tres.

Luisa: Sí, vamos a pasear por la feria y luego vamos a cenar en el restaurante argentino El Gaucho.

Germán: ...El Gaucho.

Luisa: Sí, y después de cenar todos vamos a ir al parque de diversiones para subir a la montaña rusa nueva.

Germán: ...la montaña rusa.

Luisa: Sí, sí. Muchas gracias.

Germán: De nada.

Map/Culture Activities *Argentina*

1 Argentina is the second largest country in South America and is bordered by five other countries. Locate them and write their names on the map below.

2 **Las pampas** (the fertile plains) of Argentina stretch from the Atlantic Ocean to the Andes Mountains. They are home to rich farmland, **los gauchos** (Argentine cowboys), and Argentina's capital city. Locate this city and write its name on the map.

3 South of the capital is a favorite ocean resort town of many Argentines. Find this place and write its name on the map.

_____

4 The southern part of Argentina is known as Patagonia and is characterized by harsh, dry, and sometimes extremely cold weather. Which continent, known for having a similar climate, is very near this part of Argentina?

_____

Map/Culture Activities *Argentina*

5 Are the sentences below true or false? Use the information from the cultural pages in your book to decide. Circle C for **cierto** and F for **falso**. If a sentence is false, circle the word or phrase that is incorrect and write the correct one below.

1. El dulce de leche es un postre típico de Argentina.   C   F

_____

2. César Milstein es famoso por sus conocimientos (*knowledge*) de las ciencias.   C   F

_____

3. Los gauchos argentinos trabajan en la región de Patagonia.   C   F

_____

4. El tango es un baile nuevo en Argentina.   C   F

_____

6 In the comic strip on page 352 of your book, the character Mafalda says **vos sos** instead of **tú eres**, which is a typical variation used by many Argentines. They also use vocabulary that is more or less unique to Argentina, such as the word **re** instead of **muy** to express "very." What are some variations in English, either in grammar or vocabulary, used by people where you live?

_____

_____

_____

_____

Map/Culture Activities Answer Key

ARGENTINA
Page 81

1 Refer to map above.

2 Refer to map above; Buenos Aires

3 Refer to map above.

4 Antarctica

Page 84

5

1. **C**
2. **C**
3. **F, PATAGONIA; las pampas**
4. **F, NUEVO; viejo**

6 Answers will vary.

Fine Art Activities

Colores simples, Daniel Kaplan

Many artists choose to celebrate their national identities by depicting symbols or images emblematic of their homelands. Daniel Kaplan, a young Argentine painter from Buenos Aires, has created numerous works that focus on two distinctive aspects of his country's culture: the tango and the popular vacation destination Mar del Plata. The Mar del Plata landscape is a familiar one to most Argentines. In *Colores simples,* Kaplan tries to capture this typical beach scene from a new and different perspective.

Study *Colores simples* by Daniel Kaplan and complete the following activities.

1. Study the painting in its entirety. What elements do you think the artist considers essential for an ideal beach experience? Make a list of at least five things the artist includes in the beach scene.

_____

_____

_____

_____

2. Observe the scope of the painting. How does the artist use light and detail to create the illusion of a broad expanse of seashore? Use specific examples to describe the ways in which Kaplan achieves a sense of perspective in the painting.

_____

_____

_____

_____

Colores simples (1999), Daniel Kaplan. Oil on canvas, 70 cm x 100 cm. Courtesy of Galería Zurbarán, Buenos Aires, Argentina.

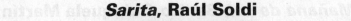

Fine Art Activities

Sarita, Raúl Soldi

Raúl Soldi is one of Argentina's most widely recognized artists. Early in his artistic career he traveled and studied in Germany, Italy, France, and the United States, where he worked as a set designer in Hollywood. He has illustrated books of poetry, and his religious art decorates famous churches from Italy to Israel. While much of his art deals with theater and performance, he also is known for his portraits and landscapes.

Complete the following activities about the painting *Sarita*, by Raúl Soldi.

1. What is the mood of this painting? What colors, images, and techniques did the artist use to create the mood? Use specific examples from *Sarita* to explain how Soldi establishes mood in his painting.

   _____

   _____

   _____

2. Examine the details of the painting and imagine what the girl is like. Write a brief story about the central figure in *Sarita*. Tell who you think she is, what she is like, and what she hopes to become.

   _____

   _____

   _____

   _____

   _____

   _____

   _____

Sarita (1947), Raúl Soldi. Oil on canvas, 74 cm x 123 cm. Courtesy of Fundación Soldi.

Fine Art Activities

Mañana de sol, Benito Quinquela Martín

Benito Quinquela Martín is one of Argentina's most popular painters and is the definitive artist of La Boca, a colorful but rough immigrant port neighborhood in Buenos Aires. Quinquela Martín was one of Argentina's first artists to focus on the urban images of Buenos Aires. He began painting portraits of his neighbors in La Boca at the age of fourteen before dedicating himself to the depiction of the surrounding cityscape. His paintings of La Boca are celebrated for their ability to relate the activity, color, and grittiness of port life.

Complete the following activities based on your analysis of *Mañana de sol*, by Benito Quinquela Martín.

1. How does Quinquela Martín create a realistic natural environment in his painting? Describe the shades and techniques used to paint water and fog in *Mañana de sol*.

_____

_____

_____

2. Select two different people from the painting and write a short history for them on the lines below. Begin by identifying where they appear in the painting, then tell what their names might be. Discuss their nationalities, the language(s) they speak, and what a typical day might involve for each.

_____

_____

_____

_____

_____

_____

_____

Mañana de sol (1966), Benito Quinquela Martín. Oleo sobre aglomerado, 77 cm x 87 cm. Courtesy of Galería Zurbarán, Buenos Aires.

Fine Art Activities

De mi Buenos Aires, Norberto Russo

Argentine Norberto Russo began his artistic career at a young age. He was a drawing teacher at eighteen, and later taught painting. It would be more than a decade, however, before Russo entered his first group exhibition and individual shows. Like the artist's other works, *De mi Buenos Aires* is characterized by Russo's careful attention to details within light and shadows. Few of his pieces portray people, yet Russo's works are notable for the warmth they convey.

Study *De mi Buenos Aires* by Norberto Russo, and answer the following questions.

1. *De mi Buenos Aires* is a realistic painting of a city street. Describe how Russo uses light and shadow and other details to achieve this effect.

_____

_____

_____

_____

2. If you were to paint a scene of your town or city, what would you paint? What landmarks or other buildings would you portray? What colors would you use? Why?

_____

_____

_____

_____

_____

_____

_____

De mi Buenos Aires (1996), Norberto Russo. Oil on canvas, Galería Zurbarán, Buenos Aires, Galería Zurbarán/SuperStock.

Fine Art Activities Answer Key

COLORES SIMPLES, DANIEL KAPLAN, p. 86

1. Answers will vary.

2. Answers will vary. The skyline is hazy and indistinct, making it appear very far away. Kaplan uses scale to achieve perspective: the numerous people on the beach become smaller, indicating distance.

SARITA, RAÚL SOLDI, p. 87

1. Answers may vary. Students should be able to provide examples to back up their answers.

2. Answers will vary.

MAÑANA DE SOL, BENITO QUINQUELA MARTÍN, p. 88

1. Answers will vary. The fog makes the background look blurry, while the viewer can see ripples and reflections in the water.

2. Answers will vary.

DE MI BUENOS AIRES, NORBERTO RUSSO, p. 89

1. Answers will vary. Possible answer: The taller building casts a shadow on the pale building and the trees in the center; the shading of the trees also suggests depth and fullness of leaves. The pedestrian walkway in the foreground is streaked with shadow and light. Cars are seen near the building, reflecting traffic.

2. Answers will vary. Students should explain their choice in their answer.

Date: _____

Dear Family:

We are about to begin *Unidad 7* of the Level 1 ¡*Avancemos*! program. It focuses on authentic culture and real-life communication using Spanish in Argentina. It practices reading, writing, listening, and speaking, and introduces students to culture typical of Argentina.

Through completing the activities, students will employ critical thinking skills as they compare the Spanish language and the culture of Argentina with their own community. They will also connect to other academic subjects, using their knowledge of Spanish to access new information. In this unit, students are learning to talk about technology, talk about a series of events, say what they did, talk about indefinite or negative situations, talk on the phone, say where they went, how it was, and what they did, and to extend invitations. They are also learning about grammar—affirmative **tú** commands, telling time, foods and beverages, preterite of regular **-ar** verbs, ¡**Qué** + adjective!, preterite of **ir, ser,** and **hacer,** and pronouns after prepositions.

Please feel free to call me with any questions or concerns you might have as your student practices reading, writing, listening, and speaking in Spanish.

Sincerely,

Family Involvement Activity

Create stories!

STEP 1

Invite your family to sit comfortably in the living room. The aim of the game is to see how well you know each other.

STEP 2

All players have to tell three stories. These stories can be about themselves, friends, or other people they know. Two of the stories have to be real and one must be invented. Each player tells all three stories, then the next player goes. The other players have to guess which story is not true for each player.

STEP 3

Try to use your Spanish in order to tell your stories. Then repeat your story in English for the group.

Write the names of the players whose false stories tricked other players:

Names

Absent Student Copymasters

Presentación / Práctica de vocabulario

Materials Checklist

☐ Student text

☐ DVD 2

☐ Video activities copymasters

☐ *Cuaderno* pages 295–297 (L1B pp. 99–101)

☐ *Cuaderno para hispanohablantes* pages 295–298 (L1B pp. 99–102)

☐ TXT CD 7 tracks 1–2

☐ L1B TXT CD 2 track 1

☐ Did You Get It? Copymasters 1 and 2

☐ ClassZone.com

Steps to Follow

☐ Study the computer vocabulary in **Presentación de vocabulario** (pp. 356–357, L1B pp. 166–168) by reading the photo captions and the accompanying text.

☐ Watch the DVD and complete the video activities copymasters.

☐ Practice the words from the **Más vocabulario** box on page 357 (L1B p. 167). Read the words aloud. Write the words in your notebook.

☐ Do **Práctica de vocabulario** on page 358 (L1B p. 169). Complete **Actividades 1** and **2**.

☐ Complete *Cuaderno* pages 295, 296, and 297 (L1B pp. 99–101).
OR
Complete *Cuaderno para hispanohablantes* pages 295, 296, 297, and 298 (L1B pp. 99–102).

☐ Check your comprehension by completing the **Para y piensa** box on page 358 (L1B p. 169).

☐ Complete Did You Get It? Copymasters 1 and 2.

If You Don't Understand . . .

☐ Watch the DVD in a quiet place. If you get lost, stop the DVD and replay it from the beginning.

☐ Listen to the CD several times without interruption. Read along in the textbook as you listen to the CD.

☐ Reread the activity directions and copy them in your own words.

☐ Use the Interactive Flashcards to help you study the lesson.

Absent Student Copymasters

Vocabulario en contexto

Materials Checklist

- [ ] Student text
- [ ] DVD 2
- [ ] Video activities copymasters
- [ ] TXT CD 7 tracks 3–4
- [ ] L1B TXT CD 2 track 2
- [ ] Did You Get It? Copymasters 1 and 3

Steps to Follow

- [ ] Study the photo on page 359 (L1B p. 170).

- [ ] Read **Cuando lees** and **Cuando escuchas** under *Strategies* on page 359 (L1B p. 170). Prepare your lists of time sequencing expressions and places Alicia's T-shirt has been.

- [ ] Watch the DVD for **Unidad 7, Telehistoria escena 1** without your book. Then watch the DVD again and complete the video activities copymasters.

- [ ] Follow along in the book as you listen to TXT CD 7 track 3. Complete the list of time sequencing expressions as you read.

- [ ] Study the words in the **También se dice** box.

- [ ] Complete **Actividades 3, 4,** and **5** (L1 p. 360, L1B p. 171).

- [ ] Write down both the questions and the answers in **Actividad 5**.

- [ ] Check your comprehension by completing the **Para y piensa** box on page 360 (L1B p. 171).

- [ ] Complete Did You Get It? Copymasters 1 and 3.

If You Don't Understand . . .

- [ ] Watch the DVD several times without interruption. Follow along in your book as you watch and listen to the DVD.

- [ ] Listen to the CD several times in a quiet place. Follow along in your book as you listen to the CD.

- [ ] Read the activity directions again and try to put them in your own words.

- [ ] Study the model and imitate it in your own answers.

- [ ] Read aloud everything that you write. Be sure that what you have written expresses what you want to say.

- [ ] If you have any questions, write them down so you can ask your teacher later.

Absent Student Copymasters

Presentación / Práctica de gramática

Materials Checklist

- [ ] Student text
- [ ] *Cuaderno* pages 298–300 (L1B pp. 102–104)
- [ ] *Cuaderno para hispanohablantes* pages 299–301 (L1B pp. 103–105)
- [ ] TXT CD 7 track 5
- [ ] Did You Get It? Copymasters 4, 5, and 11
- [ ] ClassZone.com

Steps to Follow

- [ ] Study the preterite of regular **-er** and **-ir** verbs on page 361 (L1B p. 172).
- [ ] Do **Actividades 6**, **7**, **8**, and **9** (L1 pp. 362–363, L1B pp. 173–175).
- [ ] Do **Actividades 10** and **11** (L1B p. 175).
- [ ] Listen to TXT CD 7 track 5 as you follow along in the **Pronunciación** activity on page 363 (L1B p. 174).
- [ ] Complete the *Cuaderno* pages 298, 299, and 300 (L1B pp. 102–104).
  OR
  Complete the *Cuaderno para hispanohablantes* pages 299, 300, and 301 (L1B pp. 103–105).
- [ ] Check your comprehension by completing the **Para y piensa** box on page 363 (L1B p. 175).
- [ ] Complete Did You Get It? Copymasters 4, 5, and 11.

If You Don't Understand . . .

- [ ] Listen to the CD as many times as you need.
- [ ] Reread the directions for the activity you find difficult. Write the directions in your own words.
- [ ] Study the model. Try to follow the model in your own answers.
- [ ] Read aloud everything that you write. Be sure that you understand what you are reading.
- [ ] If you have any questions, write them down for your teacher.
- [ ] If the activity has parts for two people, practice both parts.
- [ ] Use the Animated Grammar to help you understand.
- [ ] Use the Leveled Grammar Practice on the @Home Tutor.

Absent Student Copymasters

UNIDAD 7 Lección 1

Absent Student Copymasters

Gramática en contexto

Materials Checklist

- [ ] Student text
- [ ] DVD 2
- [ ] Video activities copymasters
- [ ] TXT CD 7 track 6
- [ ] Did You Get It? Copymasters 4 and 6

Steps to Follow

- [ ] Study the photo on page 364 (L1B p. 176).
- [ ] Read **Cuando lees** and **Cuando escuchas** under *Strategies* on page 364 (L1B p. 176).
- [ ] Read the script and try to understand the dialogue based on the picture. Complete the **Cuando lees** activity by practicing words and phrases about the Internet.
- [ ] Watch the DVD for **Unidad 7**, **Telehistoria escena 2** without your book. Then watch the DVD again and complete the video activities copymasters.
- [ ] Follow along in the book as you listen to TXT CD 7 track 6. Use the picture and context to help you understand the dialogue.
- [ ] Complete **Actividades 10** and **11** (L1 p. 365).
- [ ] Complete **Actividades 12** and **13** (L1B p. 177).
- [ ] Check your comprehension by completing the **Para y piensa** box on page 365 (L1B p. 177).
- [ ] Complete Did You Get It? Copymasters 4 and 6.

If You Don't Understand . . .

- [ ] Watch the DVD in a quiet place. If you get lost, rewind the scene and replay it from the beginning.
- [ ] Listen to the CD several times without interruption. Follow along in your book while you listen.
- [ ] Reread your answers to the questions to make sure they express what you want to say.
- [ ] If you have any questions, write them down for your teacher to answer later.

Absent Student Copymasters

Presentación / Práctica de gramática

Materials Checklist

- [ ] Student text
- [ ] *Cuaderno* pages 301–303 (L1B pp. 105–107)
- [ ] *Cuaderno para hispanohablantes* pages 302–305 (L1B pp. 106–109)
- [ ] Did You Get It? Copymasters 7 and 8
- [ ] ClassZone.com

Steps to Follow

- [ ] Study affirmative and negative words on page 366 (L1B p. 178).
- [ ] Do **Actividades 12**, **13**, and **14** (L1 pp. 367–368).
- [ ] Do **Actividades 14**, **15**, **16**, **17**, and **19** (L1B pp. 179–181).
- [ ] Complete *Cuaderno* pages 301, 302, and 303 (L1B pp. 105–107).
  OR
  Complete *Cuaderno para hispanohablantes* pages 302, 303, 304, and 305 (L1B pp. 106–109).
- [ ] Check your comprehension by completing the **Para y piensa** box on page 368 (L1B p. 181).
- [ ] Complete Did You Get It? Copymasters 7 and 8.

If You Don't Understand . . .

- [ ] Make sure you are in an area where you can concentrate.
- [ ] Reread the directions for the activity you find difficult. Write the directions in your own words.
- [ ] Write the model on your paper. Try to follow the model in your own answers.
- [ ] Read aloud everything that you write. Be sure that you understand what you are reading.
- [ ] Write down any questions you have for your teacher.
- [ ] If the activity has parts for two people, practice both parts.
- [ ] Think about what you are trying to say when you write a sentence. After you write your sentence, check to make sure that it says what you wanted to say.
- [ ] Use the Animated Grammar to help you understand.
- [ ] Use the Leveled Grammar Practice on the @Home Tutor.

Absent Student Copymasters

Level 1 pp. 369–371
Level 1B pp. 182–184

Todo junto

Materials Checklist

☐ Student text

☐ DVD 2

☐ Video activities copymasters

☐ *Cuaderno* pages 304–305 (L1B pp. 108–109)

☐ *Cuaderno para hispanohablantes* pages 306–307 (L1B pp. 110–111)

☐ Did You Get It? Copymasters 7 and 9

☐ TXT CD 7 tracks 7–9

☐ L1B TXT CD 2 tracks 3–4

☐ WB CD 4 tracks 1–4

☐ HL CD 2 tracks 17–20

Steps to Follow

☐ Look at the photos on page 369 (L1B p. 182) and try to figure out what is happening in them.

☐ Read the **Cuando lees** and **Cuando escuchas** sections of *Strategies* on page 369 (L1B p. 182). Copy the questions from **Cuando lees**.

☐ Review the content of **Unidad 7, Telehistoria escena 1** and **escena 2**.

☐ Watch the DVD for **Unidad 7, Telehistoria escena 3** without your book. Then watch the DVD again and complete the video activities copymasters.

☐ Follow along in the book as you listen to TXT CD 7 track 7. Use the pictures and context to help you understand the dialogue. Answer the questions in **Cuando lees**.

☐ Complete **Actividades 16, 17, 18, 19**, and **20** (L1 pp. 370–371). Complete **Actividad 18** by writing your own article about a real or imagined event at school.

☐ Complete **Actividades 20, 21, 22, 23**, and **24** (L1B pp. 183–184). Complete **Actividad 22** by writing your own article about a real or imagined event at school.

☐ Complete *Cuaderno* pages 304 and 305 (L1B pp. 108–109).
OR
Complete *Cuaderno para hispanohablantes* pages 306 and 307 (L1B pp. 110–111).

☐ Check your comprehension by completing the **Para y piensa** box on page 371 (L1B p. 184).

☐ Complete Did You Get It? Copymasters 7 and 9.

UNIDAD 7 Lección 1

Absent Student Copymasters

Absent Student Copymasters

Lectura y Conexiones

Materials Checklist

☐ Student text

☐ TXT CD 7 track 10

Steps to Follow

☐ Read **Strategy: Leer** (L1 p. 372, L1B p. 186).

☐ Read **Un cuestionario sobre las computadoras** on pages 372 and 373 (L1B pp. 186–187).

☐ Follow along with the text on TXT CD 7 track 10.

☐ Try to complete the questionnaire.

☐ Check your comprehension by completing the **¿Comprendiste?** and **¿Y tú?** sections of the **Para y piensa** box on page 373 (L1B p. 187).

☐ Read **Los juegos de lenguaje** on page 374 (L1B p. 188).

☐ Read **Las ciencias sociales**. Try to answer the questions.

☐ Read **La geografía**. Write the paragraph it describes.

☐ Read **Las ciencias** and do the research and writing.

If You Don't Understand . . .

☐ Make sure you are in an area where you can concentrate.

☐ Reread the directions for the activity you find difficult. Write the directions in your own words.

☐ Write the model on your paper. Try to follow the model in your own answers.

☐ If you have any questions, write them down so you can ask your teacher later.

☐ Practice both parts of any partner activities.

☐ Think about what you are trying to say when you write a sentence. After you write your sentence, check to make sure that it says what you wanted to say.

Absent Student Copymasters

UNIDAD 7 Lección 1

Absent Student Copymasters

Repaso de la lección

Materials Checklist

☐ Student text

☐ *Cuaderno* pages 306–317 (L1B pp. 110–121)

☐ *Cuaderno para hispanohablantes* pages 308–316 (L1B pp. 112–121)

☐ TXT CD 7 track 11

☐ L1B TXT CD 2 track 5

☐ WB CD 4 tracks 5–10

Steps to Follow

☐ Read the bullet points under **¡Llegada!** on page 376 (L1B p. 190).

☐ Complete **Actividades 1**, **2**, **3**, **4**, and **5** (L1 pp. 376–377, L1B pp. 190–191).

☐ Complete *Cuaderno* pages 306, 307, and 308 (L1B pp. 110–112).

☐ Complete *Cuaderno* pages 309, 310, and 311 (L1B pp. 113–115).
OR
Complete *Cuaderno para hispanohablantes* pages 308, 309, 310, and 311 (L1B pp. 112–115).

☐ Complete *Cuaderno* pages 312, 313, and 314 (L1B pp. 116–118).
OR
Complete *Cuaderno para hispanohablantes* pages 312, 313, and 314 (L1B pp. 116–118).

☐ Complete *Cuaderno* pages 315, 316, and 317 (L1B pp. 119–121).
OR
Complete *Cuaderno para hispanohablantes* pages 315, 316, and 317 (L1B pp. 119–121).

If You Don't Understand . . .

☐ For activities that require the CD, listen to it in a quiet place. If you get lost, stop the CD and go back.

☐ Do the activities you understand first.

☐ Review the activity directions and study the model. Try to follow the model in your own answers.

☐ Read aloud everything that you write. Be sure that you understand what you are reading.

☐ If you have any questions, write them down for your teacher to answer later.

Absent Student Copymasters

Presentación / Práctica de vocabulario

Materials Checklist

☐ Student text

☐ DVD 2

☐ Video activities copymasters

☐ *Cuaderno* pages 318–320 (L1B pp. 122–124)

☐ *Cuaderno para hispanohablantes* pages 318–321 (L1B pp. 122–125)

☐ TXT CD 7 tracks 12–13

☐ L1B TXT CD 2 track 6

☐ Did You Get It? Copymasters 13 and 14

☐ ClassZone.com

Steps to Follow

☐ Study the computer vocabulary in **Presentación de vocabulario** (pp. 380–381, L1B pp. 194–196) by reading the photo captions and the accompanying text.

☐ Practice the words from the **Más vocabulario** box on page 381 (L1B p. 194). Read the words aloud, then write them in your notebook.

☐ Watch the DVD and complete the video activities copymasters.

☐ Complete **Actividades 1** and **2** of **Práctica de vocabulario** (L1 p. 382, L1B p. 197).

☐ Complete *Cuaderno* pages 318, 319, and 320 (L1B pp. 122–124).
OR
Complete *Cuaderno para hispanohablantes* pages 318, 319, 320, and 321 (L1B pp. 122–125).

☐ Check your comprehension by completing the **Para y piensa** box on page 382 (L1B p. 197).

☐ Complete Did You Get It? Copymaster, pages 13 and 14.

If You Don't Understand . . .

☐ Watch the DVD several times in a quiet place. Go back and review the scene until you understand it.

☐ Listen to the CD in a quiet place. If you get lost, stop the CD and listen to the section again.

☐ Use the Interactive Flashcards to help you study the lesson.

UNIDAD 7 Lección 2

Absent Student Copymasters

Absent Student Copymasters

Level 1 pp. 383–384
Level 1B pp. 198–199

Vocabulario en contexto

Materials Checklist

☐ Student text

☐ DVD 2

☐ Video activities copymasters

☐ TXT CD 7 track 14

☐ Did You Get It? Copymasters 13, 14, and 22

Steps to Follow

☐ Study the photos on page 383 (L1B p. 198) for clues about meaning.

☐ Read **Cuando lees** and **Cuando escuchas** on page 383 (L1B p. 198). Prepare a map of the park per the instructions in **Cuando lees**.

☐ Read the dialogue on page 383 (L1B p. 198) and use the information to complete the **Cuando lees** map.

☐ Watch the DVD for **Unidad 7**, **Telehistoria escena 1** without your book. Then watch the DVD again and complete the video activities copymasters.

☐ Follow along in the book as you listen to TXT CD 7 track 14. Use the pictures and context to help you understand the dialogue.

☐ Study the words in the **También se dice** box.

☐ Complete **Actividades 3** and **4** (L1 p. 384, L1B p. 199).

☐ To complete **Actividad 4**, write to a friend describing the amusement park and inviting him or her to accompany you.

☐ Check your comprehension by completing the **Para y piensa** box on page 384 (L1B p. 199).

☐ Complete Did You Get It? Copymasters 13, 14, and 22.

If You Don't Understand . . .

☐ Watch the video several times. Use your textbook to help you follow along with the dialogue.

☐ Listen to the CD in a quiet place. You may need to listen several times and follow along in your book.

☐ Reread the activity directions and copy them in your own words.

Absent Student Copymasters

Presentación / Práctica de gramática

Materials Checklist

☐ Student text

☐ *Cuaderno* pages 321–323 (L1B pp. 125–127)

☐ *Cuaderno para hispanohablantes* pages 322–324 (L1B pp. 126–128)

☐ TXT CD 7 track 15

☐ L1B TXT CD 2 track 7

☐ Did You Get It? Copymasters 16 and 17

☐ ClassZone.com

Steps to Follow

☐ Study the preterite of **ir**, **ser**, and **hacer** on page 385 (L1B p. 200).

☐ Do **Actividades 5**, **6**, **7**, and **8** (L1 pp. 386–387, L1B pp. 201–202).

☐ Do **Actividades 9** and **10** (L1B pp. 202–203).

☐ Complete *Cuaderno* pages 321, 322, and 323 (L1B pp. 125–127).
OR
Complete *Cuaderno para hispanohablantes* pages 322, 323, and 324
(L1B pp. 126–128).

☐ Check your comprehension by completing the **Para y piensa** box on page 387
(L1B p. 203).

☐ Complete Did You Get It? Copymasters 16 and 17.

If You Don't Understand . . .

☐ Make sure you are in an area where you can concentrate.

☐ Reread the directions for the activity you find difficult. Write the directions in your
own words.

☐ Write the model on your paper. Try to follow the model in your own answers.

☐ If you are having trouble with an activity, complete the ones you can do first.

☐ Practice both parts of any partner activities.

☐ Use the Animated Grammar to help you understand.

☐ Use the Leveled Grammar Practice on the @Home Tutor.

Absent Student Copymasters

Gramática en contexto

Materials Checklist

☐ Student text

☐ DVD 2

☐ Video activities copymasters

☐ TXT CD 7 tracks 16–17

☐ Did You Get It? Copymasters 16 and 18

Steps to Follow

☐ Try to determine what is going on in the photo on page 388 (L1B p. 204).

☐ Read the **Cuando lees** and **Cuando escuchas** sections of *Strategies* on page 388 (L1B p. 204). Copy the questions from **Cuando escuchas** in your notebook.

☐ Read the script and try to understand the dialogue based on the picture. Write down your answers for the **Cuando lees** activity.

☐ Watch the DVD for **Unidad 7**, **Telehistoria escena 2** without your book. Then watch the DVD again and complete the video activities copymasters.

☐ Follow along in the book as you listen to TXT CD 7 track 16. Use the picture and context to help you understand the dialogue.

☐ Study the words in the **También se dice** box.

☐ Complete **Actividades 9** and **10** (L1 p. 389). Complete **Actividad 10** by writing a short description of each place listed in the box.

☐ Complete **Actividades 11** and **12** (L1B p. 205). Complete **Actividad 12** by writing a short description of each place listed.

☐ Listen to TXT CD 7 track 17 as you follow along in the **Pronunciación** activity on page 389 (L1B p. 205).

☐ Check your comprehension by completing the **Para y piensa** box on page 389 (L1B p. 205).

☐ Complete Did You Get It? Copymasters 16 and 18.

If You Don't Understand . . .

☐ Go to a quiet place to watch the DVD. If you get lost, stop the DVD and replay the scene until you understand it.

☐ Listen to the CD in a quiet place. If you get lost, stop the CD and replay the track until you understand it.

☐ Reread the activity directions and copy them in your own words.

UNIDAD 7 Lección 2

Absent Student Copymasters

Unidad 7, Lección 2
Absent Student Copymasters

104

¡Avancemos! 1
Unit Resource Book

Absent Student Copymasters

Presentación / Práctica de gramática

Materials Checklist

☐ Student text

☐ *Cuaderno* pages 324–326 (L1B pp. 128–130)

☐ *Cuaderno para hispanohablantes* pages 325–328 (L1B pp. 129–132)

☐ Did You Get It? Copymasters 19 and 20

☐ ClassZone.com

Steps to Follow

☐ Study pronouns after prepositions on page 390 (L1B p. 206).

☐ Do **Actividades 11**, **12**, **13**, and **14** (L1 pp. 391–392).

☐ Do **Actividades 13**, **14**, **15**, **16**, **17**, and **18** (L1B pp. 207–209).

☐ Complete *Cuaderno* pages 324, 325, and 326 (L1B pp. 128–130).
OR
Complete *Cuaderno para hispanohablantes* pages 325, 326, 327, and 328
(L1B pp. 129–132).

☐ Check your comprehension by completing the **Para y piensa** box on page 392
(L1B p. 209).

☐ Complete Did You Get It? Copymasters 19 and 20.

If You Don't Understand . . .

☐ Reread the directions for the activity you find difficult. Write the directions in your
own words.

☐ Write the model on your paper. Try to follow the model in your own answers.

☐ Read aloud everything that you write. Be sure that you understand what you
are reading.

☐ Write down any questions you have for your teacher.

☐ If the activity has parts for two people, practice both parts.

☐ Use the Animated Grammar to help you understand.

☐ Use the Leveled Grammar Practice on the @Home Tutor.

Absent Student Copymasters

UNIDAD 7 Lección 2

Absent Student Copymasters

Todo junto

Materials Checklist

- [ ] Student text
- [ ] DVD 2
- [ ] Video activities copymasters
- [ ] *Cuaderno* pages 327–328 (L1B pp. 131–132)
- [ ] *Cuaderno para hispanohablantes* pages 329–330 (L1B pp. 133–134)
- [ ] TXT CD 7 tracks 18–20
- [ ] L1B TXT CD 2 tracks 8–9
- [ ] WB CD 4 tracks 11–14
- [ ] Did You Get It? Copymasters 19 and 21

Steps to Follow

- [ ] Read **Cuando lees** and **Cuando escuchas** under *Strategies* on page 393 (L1B p. 210).

- [ ] Review the content of **Unidad 7, Telehistoria escena 1** and **escena 2**.

- [ ] Watch the DVD for **Unidad 7, Telehistoria escena 3** without your book. Then watch the DVD again and complete the video activities copymasters.

- [ ] Read along in your book as you listen to TXT CD 7 track 18. Use the pictures and context to help you understand the dialogue.

- [ ] Complete **Actividades 15, 16, 17, 18,** and **19** (L1 pp. 394–395). Use the instructions in **Actividad 17** to write a dialogue about one of the two topics listed or about one of your own.

- [ ] Complete **Actividades 19, 20, 21, 22,** and **23** (L1B pp. 211–212). Use the instructions in **Actividad 21** to write a dialogue about one of the two topics listed or about one of your own.

- [ ] Complete *Cuaderno* pages 327 and 328 (L1B pp. 131–132).
  OR
  Complete *Cuaderno para hispanohablantes* pages 329 and 330 (L1B pp. 133–134).

- [ ] Check your comprehension by completing the **Para y piensa** box on page 395 (L1B p. 212).

- [ ] Complete Did You Get It? Copymasters 19 and 21.

Absent Student Copymasters

Lectura cultural

Materials Checklist

☐ Student text

☐ TXT CD 7 track 21

Steps to Follow

☐ Read **Strategy: Leer** (L1 p. 396, L1B p. 214).

☐ Read **Museos excepcionales** on pages 396 and 397 (L1B pp. 214–215).

☐ Look at the photos and reread the text.

☐ Follow along with the text on TXT CD 7 track 21.

☐ Check your comprehension by completing the **¿Comprendiste?** and **¿Y tú?** sections of the **Para y piensa** box on page 397 (L1B p. 215).

If You Don't Understand . . .

☐ Listen to the CD in a quiet place. If you get lost, stop the CD and go back.

☐ Review the directions for the activity you find difficult. Write the directions in your own words.

☐ If you have any questions, write them down so you can ask your teacher later.

☐ Think about what you are trying to say when you write a sentence. After you write your sentence, check to make sure that it says what you wanted to say.

Absent Student Copymasters

Proyectos culturales

Materials Checklist

☐ Student text

Steps to Follow

☐ Read **Instrumentos de Puerto Rico y Perú** and look at the pictures (L1 p. 398).

☐ Create your own percussion instruments in **Proyecto 1**.

☐ Create your own **zampoña** in **Proyecto 2**.

☐ Read **Nombres y apellidos** (L1B p. 216).

☐ Make a family tree in **Proyecto 1**.

☐ Create a photo album in **Proyecto 2**.

☐ Complete the **En tu comunidad** segment.

If You Don't Understand . . .

☐ Read the activity directions a few times, silently and then aloud.

☐ If you have any doubts or observations, write them down so you can discuss them with your teacher later.

Absent Student Copymasters

Repaso de la lección

Materials Checklist

☐ Student text

☐ *Cuaderno* pages 329–340 (L1B pp. 133–144)

☐ *Cuaderno para hispanohablantes* pages 331–340 (L1B pp. 135–144)

☐ TXT CD 7 track 22

☐ L1B TXT CD 2 track 10

☐ WB CD 4 tracks 15–20

Steps to Follow

☐ Read the bullet points under **¡Llegada!** on page 400 (L1B p. 218).

☐ Complete **Actividades 1**, **2**, **3**, **4**, and **5** (L1 pp. 400–401, L1B pp. 218–219).

☐ Complete *Cuaderno* pages 329, 330, and 331 (L1B pp. 133–135).

☐ Complete *Cuaderno* pages 332, 333, and 334 (L1B pp. 136–138).
OR
Complete *Cuaderno para hispanohablantes* pages 331, 332, and 333 (L1B pp. 135–138).

☐ Complete *Cuaderno* pages 335, 336, and 337 (L1B pp. 139–141).
OR
Complete *Cuaderno para hispanohablantes* pages 335, 336, and 337 (L1B pp. 139–141).

☐ Complete *Cuaderno* pages 338, 339, and 340 (L1B pp. 142–144).
OR
Complete *Cuaderno para hispanohablantes* pages 338, 339, and 340 (L1B pp. 142–144).

If You Don't Understand . . .

☐ Make sure you are in an area where you can concentrate.

☐ Do the activities you understand first.

☐ Reread the directions for the activity you find difficult. Write out the directions in your own words.

☐ If there is a model provided in the activity, read it and make sure you understand what you are supposed to do.

☐ Read your answers aloud to make sure they say what you wanted to say.

☐ Write down any questions you have for your teacher.

Absent Student Copymasters

Comparación cultural

Materials Checklist

☐ Student text

☐ TXT CD 7 track 23

Steps to Follow

☐ Read the directions in **Lectura y escritura** for **Actividades 1** and **2** on page 402 (L1B p. 220).

☐ Listen to TXT CD 7 track 23 as you read **¿Conoces un lugar divertido?** on page 403 (L1B p. 221).

☐ Read **Strategy: Escribir**, then begin **Actividad 2**.

☐ Complete the **Compara con tu mundo** section on page 402 (L1B p. 221).

If You Don't Understand . . .

☐ Read through all of the instructions before you begin reading the feature.

☐ Listen to the CD in a quiet place. Pause and go back as often as necessary.

☐ Look up words you don't know.

☐ Make a list of questions if you are confused or don't know how to say something. Think of what you do know how to say.

☐ Think about what you want to say before you begin writing. Read everything you write to make sure it is clear.

Absent Student Copymasters

Repaso inclusivo

Materials Checklist

☐ Student text

☐ TXT CD 7 track 24

Steps to Follow

☐ Use TXT CD 7 track 24 to complete **Actividad 1** on page 404 (L1B p. 222).
Imitate the pronunciation of the voices on the CD.

☐ Complete **Actividades 2**, **3**, **4**, **5**, **6**, and **7** (L1 pp. 404–405, L1B pp. 222–223).

If You Don't Understand . . .

☐ For **Actividad 1**, listen to the CD in a quiet place. If you get lost, pause the CD and
go back.

☐ Read the activity directions several times. Use the textbook and review the
vocabulary and verb conjugations you need to complete each activity.

☐ Write and practice the parts of both partners in all activities that call for
partner work.

☐ Think about what you want to say before you begin to write. Read aloud everything
that you write. Make sure that it makes sense.

☐ If you have any questions, write them down for your teacher to answer later.